RE-PRESENTING "JANE" SHORE

Re-Presenting "Jane" Shore analyzes the representation of the mistress of Edward IV of England, known to us as "Jane" Shore (c. 1445–c. 1527). The daughter of a well-to-do merchant, she left her merchant husband to become the king's concubine. After Edward's death, his brother, later Richard III, charged her with witchcraft and harlotry, prompting Thomas More to include her in his exposition of Richard's perfidies in *The History of Richard III*. Since then, Jane Shore has been a frequent subject of, among others, poets (Thomas Churchyard and Thomas Deloney), playwrights (Shakespeare and Nicholas Rowe), and novelists (Guy Padget and Jean Plaidy).

Scott examines the anxiety in Anglo-American culture generated when sex and politics intersect, using the case of "Jane" Shore to show how history is compromised and complicated by context. In doing so, she reveals how women continue to be deployed as symbols rather than as actors on the larger stage of the drama that is politics.

Maria M. Scott received her Ph.D. at the University of Chicago and is an Associate Professor of English at Randolph-Macon College in Ashland, Virginia.

T0347385

For Justin

Re-Presenting "Jane" Shore

Harlot and Heroine

MARIA M. SCOTT
Randolph-Macon College, USA

Routledge
Taylor & Francis Group

LONDON AND NEW YORK

First published 2005 by Ashgate Publishing

Reissued 2018 by Routledge
2 Park Square, Milton Park, Abingdon, Oxon, OX14 4RN
711 Third Avenue, New York, NY 10017, USA

Routledge is an imprint of the Taylor & Francis Group, an informa business

First issued in paperback 2018

A Library of Congress record exists under LC control number: 2004013246

Notice:
Product or corporate names may be trademarks or registered trademarks, and are used only for identification and explanation without intent to infringe.

Publisher's Note
The publisher has gone to great lengths to ensure the quality of this reprint but points out that some imperfections in the original copies may be apparent.

Disclaimer
The publisher has made every effort to trace copyright holders and welcomes correspondence from those they have been unable to contact.

ISBN 13: 978-0-815-39149-4 (hbk)
ISBN 13: 978-1-138-62249-4 (pbk)
ISBN 13: 978-1-351-15020-0 (ebk)

Contents

List of Figures   vi
Acknowledgments   vii

Introduction   1

1   "To Sleight a Thing": or, the "Real" Mistress Shore   7

2   Fatal Attractions: or, Jane Shore and the Popular Traditions   21

3   'Tis Pity She's a Whore: or, Jane Shore on the Boards   49

4   Prosaic Morality: or, Jane Shore "Explained"   69

5   Angel in the House?: or, Jane Shore Domesticated   95

6   "The More We Change …": or, Post Office, contd.   117

Bibliography   133

Index   139

List of Figures

4.1   Jane Shore in Tudor dress. The French caption translates as "Jane at the court had a heart of great virtue;/ Oh, pardon her weakness."   90

4.2   An Interview with Lord Hastings.   91

4.3   Jane Shore doing penance.   92

4.4   Jane Shore *in extremis*. The French caption translates as "You see, she who's hand was always ready to help others/ Is herself without bread and without shelter."   93

6.1   Cover art for Susan Appleyard's *The King's White Rose*.   122

6.2   Pamela Brown as Jane Shore in Olivier's *Richard III* (Criterion/Janus).   124

6.3   "Starr-Crossed Love" by Vint Lawrence (used by permission) *The New Republic* 5 October 1998.   130

Acknowledgments

I am indebted to the Walter Williams Craigie Teaching Endowment at Randolph-Macon College for generous assistance with funds for research and travel, and to the Committee on Faculty Development, for awarding me those funds. I am grateful to my editor, Erika Gaffney at Ashgate, who first approached me about publishing *Re-presenting "Jane" Shore*, and to Ann Donohue, who shepherded the manuscript through the consideration process while the former was on leave. I wish to extend my appreciation to my colleagues in the English Department at Randolph-Macon, who have honored me with their confidence and encouragement: Mark Parker, Louise Freeman, Amy Goodwin, Laura Holliday, Tom Peyser, Ted Sheckels, and Ritchie Watson. Finally, I extend thanks to Elizabeth Gruner, Gail Lea Heaton, Martha Larrimore-Jones, and the rest of the "family" at Holy Comforter Episcopal Church in Richmond, VA.

Introduction

I doubt not some shal think this woman to sleight a thing, to be written of and set amonge the remembraunces of great matters …
(Thomas More, *History of King Richard III*, 1513)

The Harlot in some Parts of her Character is a Saint.
(Review of Nicholas Rowe's *The Tragedy of Jane Shore*, 1714)

Among the many female characters who crowd the pages of history, few appeal more strongly to the imagination, or so deeply stir our emotions as the remarkable and unfortunate lady known as Jane Shore… the beauteous Jane surrounds [Edward IV] with a glamour of romance, and romance appeals irresistibly to the human mind."
(J.E. Muddock, Preface to *Jane Shore: A Romance of History*, 1905)

So there was harlot's blood in her veins after all, she thought bitterly. So be it.
(Susan Appleyard, *The King's White Rose*, 1988)

Despite the misgivings of Sir Thomas More, the 16th-century politician and historian, later canonized by the Roman Catholic Church, the legend of "this woman" has proved a remarkably durable, endlessly adaptable, subject of popular culture. A marginal figure in a major historical event—the defeat of Richard III at Bosworth Field and the inception of the Tudor dynasty—Jane[1] Shore is the anecdote lending additional spice to the already vexed mystery of Richard, last of the Plantagenet kings. Few narrators of his reign, historical or otherwise, can resist the story of the citizen's beautiful wife who became the mistress of Edward IV and suffered at the hands of his brother after her royal lover's death.

But why? What is this story's appeal, given its marginal relevance to "world historical events?"[2] Why, in the words of novelist Muddock, does "romance [appeal] irresistibly to the human mind," and what do we mean by "romance?" Why "this woman" and not Edward's legitimate wife, married in the teeth of opposition, and a powerful political player in her own right? These are the questions that arise in the face of four centuries' worth of texts of all sorts in which Jane Shore is presented and re-presented.

The following study traces these re-presentations of the Jane Shore legend. What I intend to show is the way both her adaptability in the face of social change, and her basic appeal as an erotic victim, have rendered her an enduring object of speculation and fantasy ever since the 16th century. Representations of Jane Shore provide windows through which we may observe how our culture has fluctuated over the last four hundred years, while reminding us also about our relatively persistent fascination with sex and power, and the intersection between the two.

Part of the legend's durability is doubtless due to its elasticity; that is, little enough is known of the "real" Mistress Shore that details of her story must perforce depend primarily on the teller. Indeed, until 1972, when Nicholas Barker published his painstaking registry research establishing documentary evidence of her life, the historical account of Jane Shore amounted to a four-century game of "Post Office." Beginning with Sir Thomas More, the "facts" of her life were transmitted, transformed, and elaborated through countless incarnations; and as the original message in the game is often unrecognizable by the time it reaches the end of the chain, so does Jane Shore's story undergo some startling variations.

Until Barker's publication of "The Real Jane Shore" in 1972, the only remotely "historical" documentation derived from More's *Richard III* (of which more will be said subsequently), a history penned by the Tudor propagandist Polydore Vergil, an obscure account called "The Croyden Chronicle," a couple of letters, and a brief mention in Rymer's Latin *Foedora*. However history (or in this case herstory) would have it, the story itself took on a life of its own very quickly beginning in the 16th century. Mistress Shore became the subject of ballad and poetry, drama, prose narrative, and eventually the novel. Each incarnation presents, and re-presents, a different Shore. A few (a very few) elements (some more or less factual, some apocryphal) remain constant; but variations on the theme are legion.

The sub-title of this study implies contradiction and paradox. If Jane Shore is a harlot, a sexual transgressor, how can she be a heroine? The answer is, very easily. I should acknowledge here that of course Jane Shore is not an exclusive manifestation of the harlot/heroine paradigm; history and, subsequently, popular culture are full of them.[3] What I do contend is that Jane Shore has proved infinitely adaptable to developing periodic and cultural agendae in a way that others have not. As I have argued, the very paucity of real information about Jane Shore allows the artist to mold her into whatever shape s/he wishes. She is the perfect erotic object, eternally available and infinitely exploitable. Just as the female body has often functioned as a metaphor for exploration and conquest, so is the "map" of culture delineated in the Jane Shore corpus.

It is instructive that the popular culture manifestations of Jane Shore began to appear in England at precisely the same time that the social structure was confining the parameters of love to marriage and the nuclear family. Marriage and the family as the foundation of social order is a hallmark of modern western culture, and threats to it call for narrative containment. Shore constitutes a violation of the norm, but also articulates the problematic nature of it when treated as an institution upon which the entire social order depends. Such institutions are not always at the service of the individual.[4] Thomas More, having suggested that Shore was perhaps married at an over-early age, editorializes thus:

> But forasmuche as they were coupled ere she wer wel ripe, she not very fervently loved, for whom she never longed. Which was happely the thinge, that the more easily made her encline unto ye kings appetite when he required her. (55)

This extenuation is elaborated upon over and over in representations from the 16th century through the twentieth. Representations of Shore clearly reflect their cultures' engagement with the often contradictory values of desire and social order. When the desiring subject is a monarch, and when the marriage vow he violates is in a way representative of marriage as a state institution (ensuring orderly succession and inheritance of property), the consequences of such a violation may become immense.[5] It is not a little ironic that Richard of Gloucester succeeded in displacing his nephews by, in part, questioning their legitimacy, and even the legitimacy of the late king himself.

Such narratives do more than simply address and resolve contradictory forces at work at a given moment; they provide a means for understanding them and shaping the social order's self-consciousness. In his study, *Adulterous Alliances*, Richard Helgerson writes:

> If the whole of our modern, middle-class world does not arise from the story of Jane Shore—and it surely doesn't—a fair part of its literary self-representation does…[T]his story puts the intersection of home and state at the very center of attention…If that intersection, that adulterous alliance, is, as I am arguing essential to the emergence of the domestic and bourgeois drama and painting that, since the late eighteenth century, has occupied a dominant position in Western literature and art, the story of Jane Shore comes as close as we are likely to get to providing a paradigmatic, perhaps even founding case. (34)

This is, as Helgerson himself admits, a "big claim," but I think it is essentially correct, and borne out by the following pages.

A point that Helgerson does *not* make, but which I think is essential to the pivotal nature of the legend, is that Jane Shore not only sins against the sexual conventions of her culture, but crosses social boundaries to do it. The growing wealth and subsequent power of the merchant class in the late 15th century (not to mention the monarch's increasing dependence on that wealth) precludes a simple *droit de seigneur* interpretation of the liaison. Jane Shore's transgression enacts the anxiety of a culture in transition. Her status as the daughter and wife of merchants is particularly emblematic of the capitalism that is to slowly erode aristocratic power over the next four centuries. Already in the reign of Edward IV, the goodwill of the merchant class was essential to the monarch's political—and financial—well-being (Ross, *Edward* 174, 353).[6] As it evolves, the story often, as we shall see, highlights the way changing economic relations affect views—both positive and negative—toward monarchical privilege and the autonomy of the subject. Thus the story reflects, and continues to reflect, as much caste anxiety as sexual tension in an evolving social landscape.

This social context explains an additional paradox beyond the harlot/heroine one: that is, for a story predicated on adultery, there is often precious little sex in it, at least sex *per se*. This is not only a function of the varying degrees of reticence about matters sexual in the different periods covered here, but of how representations of sexual transgression and/or engagement operate in the larger social framework. By foregrounding and controlling sexual disorder in narratives in which the good end happily and the bad unhappily (that is what fiction means),[7] such texts work to neutralize any accompanying social tensions. One can say this, of course, of any popular entertainment. Sometimes popular culture is great art; sometimes it is not. But it is always an artifact, evidence of a given community's desires (and anxieties) at a given time.[8]

Helgerson traces the legend up through Nicholas Rowe's play; I mean to bring it up to the present. Surveys of the Jane Shore literature have appeared a number of times in this century. The earliest is a dissertation in German produced by Willy Budig, for the Universität Rostock in 1908. While it details a number of the Jane Shore texts, it is a summary rather than an analysis and, interestingly, leaves out the 19th-century novel versions altogether (although unlike myself, Budig detours toward the end into French-language versions). C.J.S. Thompson's *The Witchery of Jane Shore* (1933) incorporates a number of aspects (historical and literary) of the tale, but seeks to reconcile various iterations rather than examine their differences. The most in-depth analysis appears in Esther Beith-Halahmi's 1964 monograph *Angell Fayre or Strumpet*

Lewd: Jane Shore as an Example of Erring Beauty in Sixteenth-Century Literature. As the title declares, Beith-Halami confined her study primarily to the 16th-century texts (she does make reference to Nicholas Rowe's 1714 play); moreover, her focus on "bewtie" necessarily leaves out a number of important considerations when looking at the evolution of the legend over the long term. James M. Harner's "Jane Shore in Literature: A Checklist" covers a broad spectrum of representations, but provides little in the way of analysis.

My project begins, more or less, where these leave off. I propose in this study, not only to bring together a number of different versions of the story into a holistic consideration, but also to illustrate two broader arguments. The first, which is hardly new, is that any literary-historical product reflects the specific cultural conditions in which it is produced at least as much as, if not more than the period it purports to represent. My second argument is that the long-term appeal of the story owes not a little to its engagement with sexual tension: the illicit nature of Shore's sexual status, the subsequent attraction/repulsion embedded in cultural responses to it, and its association, however marginal (or not, depending on the representation) with the rise and fall of political leaders and social change.

Jane Shore is a creature of her time or, rather I should say, times. The very way the story has adapted itself demonstrates culture's desire to express itself, to make itself coherent, in both its evolving and its enduring values and concerns. Jane Shore's transgressive sexuality is to an extent contained and controlled by the narratives about her, but these narratives also underscore the essential doubleness of her character, both sinful and saintly, and attempts to reconcile these two character types tend to end up heightening the tension between them. This doubleness is equally apparent in the historical contexts in which these narratives are produced; the more sexual desire seems to oppose social order, the more this tension is particularly visible.

Finally, narratives about Jane Shore, and about others like her,[9] also betray a (to me) dishearteningly durable susceptibility, on the part of both male and female producers of texts, to two qualities: The first is the inevitable attribution of women's power, regardless of other, more pertinent qualifications, exclusively to their sexual attractiveness and availability. The second, even more disturbing, is the erotic appeal of female victimization that persists despite social and legislative advances. Neither historians nor creative writers are immune to a kind of prurient attraction to erotic suffering . In the following pages, I hope to engage that attraction, to the end that we might be more self-conscious of the way our own re-presentations are colored by these persistent prejudices.

Notes

[1]   While Mistress Shore's given name was actually Elizabeth and not Jane, I will refer to her as she has come down to us through popular culture.

[2]   The phrase is György Lukács'. I use the terms "history" and "historical" with some reservation, since their meanings are not absolute. I will try, whenever using them, to make clear their contextual limitations.

[3]   For example, Henry II and his "fair Rosamond;" Henry VIII and Anne Boleyn; Thomas Jefferson and Sally Hemmings; Edward VIII and Mrs. Simpson; Prince Charles and Camilla Parker-Bowles; and, oh yes, Bill Clinton and Monica Lewinsky. Some of the women in these cases share with Jane Shore the *socially* transgressive element of illicit sexuality: Mrs. Simpson, for example was a divorced woman *and* an American (two strikes!). Sally Hemmings was an African American slave, thus violating both racial and proprietal norms. Jane Shore was not just a mistress, but a commoner sleeping with, and possibly influencing the public policy of, a king.

[4]   This truth is painfully evident in our own controversy over the definition of "marriage," from which some lawmakers would exclude same-gender couples who, they believe, will undermine the foundation of social order.

[5]   Freud, for example, notes that the foundation of "civilization" depends explicitly on the limitation of sexual satisfaction: "On one hand love comes into opposition to the interests of civilization; on the other, civilization threatens love with substantial restrictions" (*Civilization* 50).

[6]   Ross goes so far as to argue that "Edward IV has some claim to be regarded as the first 'merchant king' in English history" (*Edward* 351).

[7]   My apologies to Oscar Wilde.

[8]   "Yes, the story was summoned forth by tensions within the culture that craved a medium through which to express themselves. But, at the same time, the story worked to define those tensions and bring them to conscious realization. Even more than most significantly resonant stories, the story of Jane Shore helped remake the world by which it was made" (Helgerson 35).

[9]   Showtime, for example, aired in Fall 2002 an "original" movie, *Power and Beauty*. From the synopsis: "Judy is a smart, attractive woman who finds herself the object of desire for some of the most famous and powerful men of their time. Despite her pride and independence, she becomes defined by her associations with these men" (http://www.sho.com/movies)

Chapter 1

"To Sleight a Thing": or, the "Real" Mistress Shore

In the tapestry that begins Jane Shore legend, there is, necessarily, both warp and woof. The first involves the 15th-century transition between the Wars of the Roses and the inception of the Tudor dynasty, over which much historical ink has been shed and not a little bitterness provoked. While this study is the history of a legend rather than straight history, familiarity with the basic outlines of this period in England's history is useful in interpreting the subsequent re-presentations. The second component is the story of Mistress Shore herself, much of which has only recently come to light. I shall take them in that order.

I choose to begin the Wars of the Roses with an ending, the final words of the Chorus at the end of Shakespeare's *Henry V*:

> Henry the Sixt, in infant bands crown'd King
> Of France and England, did this king succeed;
> Whose state so many had the managing,
> That they lost France, and made his England bleed;
> Which oft our stage hath shown … (Epilogue 9–12)

At the conclusion of his second historical tetralogy, Shakespeare invokes his first, the three parts of *Henry VI* and *Richard III*. These four plays chronicle the unfortunate reign of the last three Plantagenet monarchs, and the subsequent emergence of the Tudor dynasty that culminated in Elizabeth I, Shakespeare's queen and sometime muse. In the early-to-mid 20th century, *the* authoritative text on this transition was John Gairdner's *History of the Life and Reign of Richard III*. Subsequent study has qualified that authority, noting that Gairdner more or less swallowed whole and regurgitated the Tudor party line initiated by Thomas More, and I have found most useful the works of Charles Ross and, to a somewhat lesser extent, Desmond Seward. I also confess a lingering affection for the highly accessible account by Thomas B. Costain in *The Last Plantagenets* and the more speculative, but still enjoyable, *Daughter of Time* by Josephine Tey. What follows is indebted to all these texts to some extent.

When "Henry the Sixt" became king, he was nine months old and the government was of necessity delegated to his Beaufort uncles, descended from Henry's great-uncle, John of Gaunt (his great-grandfather Edward III's brother) and his second wife Katherine Swynford. Henry, as an adult, appears to have been a mild-mannered, religious man, not overly concerned with politics, and somewhat overwhelmed by his anything-but-mild wife, Margaret of Anjou. Indeed, Ross calls him "the best-intentioned and the most ineffectual of all English kings" (*Edward* 11). As a matter of fact the king succumbed in 1453 to a severe nervous breakdown[1] and the kingdom fell briefly under the protectorship of his cousin, Richard, Duke of York.[2] Dashing, decisive, and dynamic, everything King Henry was not, Richard became a lightning rod for popular discontent and a challenge to the king's authority; in the late 1450s discord between the royal house of Lancaster and the upstart house of York soon erupted into armed conflict, with the combatants sporting either the Red Rose of Lancaster or the White Rose of York. Thus began the first "War of the Roses."

Richard did not live to see victory in the early spring of 1461; the spoils accrued to his son, Edward. With the assistance of the powerful Nevill family, headed by the Earl of Warwick (nick-named "King-Maker"), Edward routed the Lancastrian forces at Towton in Yorkshire, and was crowned in London the following June. "Uneasy lay the head," however. Warwick's support had to be paid for with huge rewards of influence and power. Indeed, the Earl took it upon himself to choose the young monarch's bride and negotiate the terms of the marriage. But the young king had other ideas. Edward was already known, at twenty-four, to be susceptible to female charm; after his death he was charged with at least two youthful seductions that would call into question the legitimacy of his acknowledged sons. In 1464 Edward became enamored with (some would say bewitched by) a young impoverished widow named Elizabeth Grey, neé Woodville. To add insult to injury, her husband, Sir Thomas, had died fighting for the Lancastrians, and she had two adolescent sons. Lady Grey apparently played her cards very cleverly, refusing to be seduced and insisting on nothing less than marriage. Edward complied. He took this action despite his knowledge that Warwick was pursuing negotiations for an alliance between Edward and Bona, the sister-in-law of the French King Louis. Warwick was not amused.

It is, in passing, interesting that it is Jane Shore and not Elizabeth Woodville who has survived as a popular culture heroine, given the former's minor role in the "world historical" events of the late 15th century. There is no question whatsoever as to the political power Elizabeth wielded: her uncle, brothers, and sons by her first marriage became extremely (many thought dangerously) powerful under Edward IV, and Elizabeth herself played a prominent role, after her husband's death, in the bargain with Henry, Earl of Richmond which put him on the throne in exchange for making her daughter his Queen. Suffice it to say, in the 1460s she was not only an insult to Warwick, but also a perceived threat to the hereditary nobility, who saw Woodvilles and Greys usurping honors they presumed should be reserved to themselves.

There was discontent even closer to home, too, which Warwick wasted no time in exploiting. Edward's brother George, the Duke of Clarence, was apparently ambitious and reckless, a problematic combination. Edward had withheld consent to Clarence's marriage with Warwick's daughter (a match which would have made Clarence very wealthy indeed, and perhaps a little too powerful for his brother's taste). In a startling piece of *rapprochement*, Warwick and Clarence cut a deal with Margaret of Anjou, in exile with her son and husband, to secure French support for a rebellion that would restore Henry VI—the very man Warwick the "King-maker" had fought to depose—to the English throne. The ease with which they accomplished this suggests how very unpopular indeed Edward and his queen had made themselves with the wealthy baronage, which flocked to Warwick's standard in late 1469 and toppled Edward with minimal bloodshed. It was now Edward's turn to go into exile and plot invasion.

His brother's permission no longer at issue, Clarence had married Warwick's daughter Isabel. And as part of the arrangement between Warwick and Margaret, her son Prince Edward married Warwick's *second* daughter, Anne. Thus related by marriage to both houses of York and Lancaster, the Earl had once more consolidated power to his own advantage and, for the second time in his career, "made" a king.

Henry VI's "readeption," as it is called, did not last long, however. Warwick was overly aggressive in punishing his enemies and asserting his prerogatives. Both he and Queen Margaret snubbed Clarence, who was forced to accept a much more modest reward than that which they had promised him. The popularity of Henry VI, whom most English had always considered a good man, carried little weight once it became clear that it was Warwick and the Queen who were running the government. Indeed, it was Margaret, not Henry, who rode at the head of the Lancastrian troops at the fateful battle of Tewkesbury in May 1671. Nevill had already been defeated and killed at Barnet a month before; Tewkesbury finished the rout of the Lancastrians, as Edward captured Margaret and Prince Edward was slain.

Having regained power, Edward kept it. He publicly forgave his brother Clarence, and heaped great honors and power on his youngest brother Richard, Duke of Gloucester. Although he continued to exalt the upstart Woodvilles, to the chagrin of Richard and of his Lord Chamberlain, William Hastings, and despite his questionable foreign policy, he seemed to have learned how to retain his popularity, particularly among the rising merchantocracy. His patronage of that increasingly powerful London constituency extended to the dubious compliment of taking one of its members as his mistress: the wife of one William Shore.

The daughter of a well-to-do London merchant, John Lambert, Elizabeth was born circa 1450 (Barker 386). This daughter married William Shore, also a merchant, probably at a rather young age, presumably through parental influence. At some point after her marriage, she attracted the attention of King Edward, who was popular in the City and also known for his roving eye. A petition for annulment of the Shore marriage was recorded in 1476 (Barker 387–88), citing the husband's frigidity and the wife's desire to bear children. William Shore more or less vanishes at this point, whether in humiliation or, as Thomas More would suggest, out of deference to the king.

Of Shore's position at court there is no record, unless one consults Sir Thomas More's account. While that gentleman's "history" has not fared well under critical historical scrutiny, it nevertheless suggests three reasons for Shore's enduring popularity as a character. First, More claims that she could both read and write "well," an unusual circumstance for women at the time, but perhaps less unusual in the merchant class, since women were often integral participants in their fathers'/husbands' businesses. Second, she was the "meriest" of Edward's mistresses (there were apparently three, according to More). Finally, she won praise and popularity by using her influence with her royal lover to assist worthy supplicants. She also supposedly interceded for persons who were out of favor with the king, gaining for them renewed recognition.

Regardless of the truth or fiction of these characteristics the early death of Edward at 41 seems to have prompted a radical reversal. Some narratives, including More's, have it that she transferred her favors to Edward's former Lord Chamberlain, William Hastings; some add that she also had a liaison with Thomas, Marquis of Dorset, Edward's step-son (these charges will be explored later). What we do know, though, is that the Lord Protector, Edward's brother Richard (Edward's sons were both minors) confiscated her goods and placed her under arrest, to face the charge of witchcraft (prompting Simon Stallworth's comment in a letter to his patrons, the Pastons: "Mastress Chore is in prisone: what schall happyne hyr I knowe nott" [Barker 388]). Apparently unable to make that case, Richard settled for the lesser, but more obvious charge of "impurity," Shore having indisputably lived in concubinage with at least one man not her husband, if not more. According to Ross, one of Richard's strategies in promoting his own rule was his championship of purity and virtue over vice, and Shore's conviction provided a not-so-subtle critique of the previous reign's licentiousness, not to mention of Hastings (and possibly Dorset)[3] (Ross, *Richard* 137). She was ordered to do public penance, and then apparently returned to prison.

Many of the subsequent accounts would truncate her story there: legend has it that the king (Richard having by this time deposed his nephews who mysteriously disappeared from view) was said to have issued a proclamation (not extant) that Shore be turned out of doors and that anyone who offered her harbor or nourishment would be executed. These narratives have her expiring of exposure and want very soon after her penance (often, poetically, in Shore-ditch, about which much ink has been spilt regarding its eponymous nature).

The truth, as the truth often is, is probably more prosaic. A letter from King Richard to the Bishop of London complains that his solicitor, one Thomas Lynom, has proposed marriage to Shore, still in prison. Presumably, he encountered her there on the king's business and was, as the king testily puts it, "blinded and abused" by her. There is no record of the marriage, but there exists a copy of William Lambert's will, which leaves a bed of arras to his "daughter, Elizabeth Lyneham" and some odd change to "Julyan Lyneham" (a frustratingly androgynous name) (Barker 389). There is every chance, then, that Elizabeth Lambert Shore ended her life as she began it, in relatively respectable bourgeois comfort.

Not so, of course, King Richard. He died at Bosworth Field in 1485, a mere two years into his reign. His opponent and successor was Henry Tudor, Earl of Richmond, who had fought on the Yorkist side at Tewkesbury. Descended on one side from the powerful Beaufort family and on the other from Katherine of Valois, widow of Henry V, who subsequently married (none too soon, either, it was said) Owen Tudor, Henry consolidated power by marrying the daughter of Edward IV and Elizabeth Woodville (also Elizabeth), and set into motion a monumental propaganda machine that was in its time a masterpiece of "spin."

The "official" Tudor historian was one Polydore Vergil who, with others, was "anxious to impress upon their fellow-countrymen how the establishment of the Tudor dynasty and saved England from the vicious and damaging civil conflict which had wracked the country during the quarrels between the Houses of Lancaster and York" (Ross, *Wars* 7).[4] More integral to my narrative, however, is the account penned by Sir Thomas More.

The medium was More's *History of Richard III*. The message was the vile crimes of Richard III. Never mind that More was only eight years old at the time of Bosworth Field; he had a first-hand source, Bishop Morton, who was later much exalted in the first Tudor reign. More's brief was more than just to blacken Richard for posterity; his task was to call into question the whole York dynasty's fitness to rule. This text was widely accepted for centuries, and formed the basis of many popular texts, of which Shakespeare's *Richard III* is the most famous. Parts of Shakespeare's play are dramatized straight from More's *Richard*, including the famous (or infamous) murder of the princes, Edward's sons, on Richard's orders. Written during the reign of "Gloriana," Queen Elizabeth, Henry VII's granddaughter, Shakespeare's play culminated the century-long vilification of Richard and consecration of the Tudor dynasty as fulfilled in Elizabeth.

One aspect of this vilification is Richard's treatment of his brother's former mistress. It is therefore imperative to examine More's document carefully as it pertains to Mistress Shore, since it set the standard for the majority of accounts to come.

"To sleight a thing:" Mistress Shore and Thomas More

> I doubt not some shal think this woman to sleight a thing, to be written of and set amonge the remembraunces of great matters: which thei shal specially think, that happely shal esteme her only by that thei now see her. (More 56)

The text is More's famous—and infamous—*History of Richard III*. Whatever the historical merits or demerits of the text may be, it is the closest to contemporary account of the woman known as Jane Shore. I would like to highlight More's own question here: why, indeed, does he choose to include so "sleight" a thing, an adulterous wife, plaything of a king, in his narrative of political intrigue and Tudor propaganda?

Shore is not, of course, the only politically influential woman in More's *Richard*. Edward's queen, Elizabeth Woodville, is also a compelling presence, a woman who presumes to play in a man's game of dynasty-building. It is certainly true that Elizabeth's power was significant, and of course it survived Edward's death, which Mistress Shore's did not. Alan Clarke

Shepard has suggested that the critical attention Shore has received is due to her "complicitous adultery" which "is more luridly fascinating to us than is Elizabeth's defiant political resistance to men's demands" (313). Shepard goes on to argue that while More's account of Elizabeth seeks to valorize her transgression, the account of Shore merely reinscribes her in a masculinist discourse in which women are sexual objects (314). "Shore's tragedy," he writes, "is that she lives out the class and gender inequities that allow her to be a victim of Edward's 'abuse'" (315).

Exactly. But what Clarke fails explicitly to acknowledge is the fact that Shore appears to constitute enough of a threat to that masculinist discourse to require such reinscription, while Elizabeth Woodville does not. Both Shore and Elizabeth appear to transgress gender norms, but only Shore violates the norms of social status as well. This is why, although there is reason to believe that Mistress Shore became once more a respectable married woman, More finds it necessary to assure us that "at this day shee beggeth of many at this daye living" (57), and to comment on the decline in her physcial appearance (55). This is not merely a "reinscription" of Mistress Shore into her city-merchant origins; More's exemplum suggests that one who wields power against both gender and social norms can expect, not just "reinscription," but utter degradation. Clearly Mistress Shore constitutes a threat to order, both gender and social, that surpasses Elizabeth's.

The flip side to her transgression, however, is Edward's apparent acceptance of her advice and influence. If a woman's trespass into the political realm in a sense un-womans her, then a man's—particularly a monarch's—acquiescence in that trespass must effeminate, or un-man, him. Thus, we can also see Mistress Shore's story as an implicit criticism of the Yorkist monarch who, by privileging the counsel of a woman who is also a commoner, violates distinctions that are the foundation of social order. Moreover, the explicitly sexual nature of her influence makes her, in the words of Constance Jordan, an "unofficially powerful woman" (213), as opposed to Elizabeth Woodville, whose power as Queen was, if not popular, at least "official."

More's own position on "political feminism" (Jordan 202) is vague. The "syphogrants" of Utopia are all, presumably, male, as is the governor (123, 143), and domestic authority follows patriarchal order (191). Women voluntarily join their husbands in battle, but in a clearly ancillary position (209–11). In what seems a radical move, More allows Utopian women to function as priests, but only a few, and only those who, significantly, are "widow[s] advanced in years" (229), suggesting that women who may still be sexually active are unsuitable for positions of power. From this we may infer that in More's ideal world only women who have ceased to function as sexual agents may be trusted to wield public power independently. However, More's opinion on female political agency is only secondary; my concern here is More's opinion of an annointed monarch's vulnerability to the "unofficial," explicitly sexual influence of a woman who neither by birth or marital status had any legitimate claim to such influence.

At the beginning of *Richard III*, More describes Edward IV glowingly as

> a goodly parsonage, and very Princely to behold, of hearte couragious, politique in consaile, in adversitie nothynge abashed, in prosperitie, rather ioyfull then prowde, in peace iust and merficul, in warre, sharpe and fyerce, in the field, bold and hardye, and natheless no farther then wysdome woulde, adventurouse. . . He was of visage lovelye, of bodye mightie, stronge, and cleane made: howe bee it in his latter dayes wyth over liberall dyet, somewhat corpulente and boorelye [sic], and natheless not uncomelye, hee was of youthe greatelye geven to fleshlye wantonnesse: from which healthe of bodye in great prosperitye and Fortune, wythout a specyall grace hardilye refrayneth. (4)

This passage describes an attractive man, well-loved by the people, despite the not unusual circumstances of Edward's "attaynyng the Crowne by battayle" (3) and his carnal habits. More notes, at the same time, that nostalgia for Edward is partly a reaction to the "crueltie, mischiefe, and trouble of the tempestuous worlde that followed" (4). Despite Edward's attractiveness, then, More subtly qualifies his praise.

Later in his account, More states that Richard charges Hastings, Edward's Lord Chamberlain, of having corrupted the late king with his "evyl company, sinister procuring, and ungracious ensample, as well in many other thinges as in the vicious living and indordinate abusion of his body, both with many other, and also specialli with shores wife" (53). This is More's first reference to Mistress Shore who, according to More, became Hastings' paramour after Edward's death. She is next invoked as the subject of Richard's "covetise" (54) and spurious accusation of witchcraft. The Protector "spoiled her of al yet she ever had, about the value of ii or iii M. marks, and sent her body to prison" (54). Unable to make the witchcraft charge stick, says More, Richard then "layd heinously to her charge, the thing that herself could not deny, that all the world wist was true, and that natheles every man laughed at to here it then so sodainly so highly taken, that she was nought of her body" (54). He goes on to describe the public penance Richard imposed upon Shore, in a highly sympathetic manner, "In which she went in countenance and pace demure so womanly" (54), that "many good folke also that hated her living, and glad were to se sin corrected: yet pitied thei more her penance, then reioyced therein, when thei considerd that the protector procured it, more of a corrupt intent then any vertuous affeccion" (55).

More claims Richard took these actions with "corrupt intent": the public humiliation of Jane Shore served to support the contention that Edward was a profligate, which would make more likely the illegitimacy of his sons. And of Edward's three mistresses, Shore was left the most vulnerable to such proceedings by Edward's death, being of common stock while the other two "were somwhat greter parsonages" (56). Again, she had violated social distinction as well as the rule of chastity.

Lee Cullen Khanna posits that More presents Jane Shore (and Elizabeth Woodville) as "Richard's victims, but even more importantly, his moral opposites" (45). However, if More's interest in Shore had been confined solely to King Richard's abuse for political purposes, he would have had nothing much more to say about her. Instead, immediately after this passage he launches into her background, describing her upbringing, her marriage ("somewhat to sone"), and her persuasion with "hope of gay apparel, ease, plesur and other wanton welth" (55) to become Edward's concubine. He challenges those who say she was never pretty; they are judging her, he argues, on the basis of her appearance in old age, "(for she yet liveth)" at the time he is writing. However, More asserts that Shore's beauty was secondary to her personality: "For a proper wit had she, and could both rede well and write, mery in company, redy and quick of aunswer, neither mute nor ful of bable, sometime taunting without displesure and not without disport" (56). This sounds less like criticism of a "fallen woman" and more like praise of an ideal courtier. More further distinguishes Shore from Edward's other two mistresses as the "meriest," in whom the king "therefore toke speciall pleasure." Edward's favor,

> ... to saith trouth (for sinne it wer to belie the devil) she never abused to any mans hurt, but to many a mans comfort and relief: where the king toke displeasure, she would mitigate and appease his mind: where men were out of favour, she would bring them in his grace. For many that had highly offended, shee obtained pardon. Of great forfetures she gate men remission. And finally in many weighty sutes, she stode many men in gret stede, either for none, or very smal rewardes, and those rather gay then rich: either for that she was content with the dede selfe well done, or for that she delited to be suid unto, and to show what she was able to do with the king, or for that wanton women and welthy be not alway covetouse. (56)

The tension in this passage is apparent. Shore may be "the devil," but she clearly possesses great charm and sympathy in More's eyes. He says that she "abused" the king's favor only for good (can it still then properly be called abuse?). More provides hints about the kind of influence Shore wielded in the language he uses. She obtained pardon for those that "highly" offended; she obtained remission of "grete" forfeitures; and she supported "many men" in "weighty" suits. Interestingly, this kind of advocacy would much more appropriately be practiced by the legitimate queen,[5] but More makes no mention of intercessory interventions on the part of Elizabeth.

In the end, More seems unable to draw a final conclusion as to her motives for do-goodery, but all of his alternatives are interesting. He first suggests that "the dede selfe well done" was ample reward to Jane Shore for her interventions. This is a conclusion that many subsequent literary representations also draw. Thomas Heywood's Shore, c. 1599, for instance, rationally asserts that though "For all my good cannot redeeme my ill;/ Yet to doe good I will endevour still" (82). In subsequent accounts in the 19th and 20th centuries, Shore becomes a self-appointed voice of moderation, restraining King Edward from fleshly overindulgence and recalling him to his royal duties. The second of More's explanations is even more interesting: that she liked to show "what she was able to do wyth the king." While making Shore seem less altruistic, this suggestion also raises serious questions: Could Edward's mistress wrap the king around her little finger and get him to do anything she wanted? Was the ruler of England in thrall to a common merchant's wife who was no better than she should be? More ends this speculation rather lamely with the proposal that "wanton women and welthy be not always covetouse."

Why would More want to emphasize Shore's influence? And why would he then waffle on the subject of her motivation? First of all, More is not so much interested in Shore's motivation as in her rhetorical function. Leonard Dean, in his literary analysis of *Richard III*, identifies in the rhetorical styles employed by More a very deliberate agenda. He writes, "More was working as an artist and a teacher rather than as a scholar" (28), and goes on to detail some of the classical literary models upon which More drew. One of More's chief teacher's aids, claims Dean, was irony. For example, the passage in which Shore is declared "nought of her body" is meant, argues Dean, to provoke a smile from the reader as a piece of delicate sarcasm. We are to see Richard as grabbing at straws to discredit Shore with her "shocking" lifestyle that was certainly a shock to no one at court (30). In this later passage More subtly undermines Edward's integrity by reminding the reader "what [Shore] was able to do wyth the king." Although More's earlier encomiums on Edward appear devoid of irony, is there not something ironic in a king's manipulation by his sex toy? A politically astute Tudor reader, conditioned to the absolutism displayed by Henry VII, would certainly understand such influence as pernicious, regardless of the beneficial results, and censure the king for putting himself in so undignified a position. More has no trouble attributing motives to his characters for their bad deeds; Jane Shore is an exception in the narrative in that she is commended for good deeds and at the same time robbed of full moral credit for them by More's ambiguous language.

At the end of this account, More seems to call its relevance into question, or presume that his readers might:

> I doubt not some shal think this woman to sleight a thing, to be written of and set amonge the remembraunces of great matters: which thei shal specially think, that happely shal esteme her only by that thei now see her. But…[h]er doinges were not much lesse, albeit thei be muche less remembred, because thei were not so evil. For men use if they have an evil turne, to write it in marble: and whoso doth us a good tourne, we write it in duste which is not worst proved by her. (56–7)

The last sentence clearly reveals part of More's didactic purposes in devoting so much attention to Jane Shore: he wishes to illustrate the moral point that "The evil that men do lives after them;/ The good is oft interréd with their bones." She is also an example of how the mighty are fallen. In order to make this second point, however, he has to emphasize the power she once had and maximize her present degradation. It is rather remarkable, though, that More quite deliberately invokes a male paradigm rather than a female one (there is no explicit comparison, for example, with Elizabeth Woodville in the Shore material); indeed, the passage seems to recall his earlier leave-taking of Lord Hastings:

> Thus ended this honorable man, a good knight and a gentle, of gret aucthorite with his prince, of living somewhat dessolate, plaine and open to his enemy, and secret to his frend: eth to begile, as he that of good hart and corage forestudied no perilles. A loving man and passing well beloved. Very faithful, and trusty ynough, trusting to much. (52)

The admirable qualities, mingled with the weaknesses, make Hastings, like Shore, seem more attractive than venal and make both serve as moral examples of the vulnerability of one's body and soul to evildoers like Richard as a result of "dessolate" living in both cases.

More cannot wholly approve of Hastings, who was a supporter of the Yorkist succession, but he can make Hastings' downfall seem a product of weakness rather than evil. The same is true of Jane Shore; while he laments her adultery, he also admits that she probably didn't have a very good marriage, and that her seduction was a result of a weakness for gaiety rather than lust. More further mitigates his criticism of Shore with his account of her positive influence on the king. And as with Lord Hastings, his summation of her story emphasizes her admirable rather than "sinful" qualities. Jane Shore, like Hastings, was betrayed by her weaknesses into wrongdoing, therefore making punishment, but not condemnation, inevitable.

At the same time, though, Shore is distinguishable from Hastings by more than gender. Khanna argues that the old-age suffering More attributes to Shore "is not to be seen as just retribution for promiscuity (as others, less sympathetic to women than Thomas More, might have interpreted it) but as a comment on the problems of the virtuous in this world" (47). I would like to complicate this claim by suggesting that more than "virtue" is at issue here (after all, Elizabeth Woodville is also a virtuous foil to Richard, but does not end, in More's account, so badly). While Hastings can die a martyr's death at the hands of Richard, and Elizabeth can retire quietly to a religious house, Edward's commoner mistress merits no such distinction, living on, but in poverty and obscurity, a sad reminder to all who would challenge the social order.

It is impossible to argue the literal "truth" of More's account even of Jane Shore, since More's political agenda was his primary concern and he needed to reconcile "truth" with that agenda. However, this is the first comprehensive portrait of "Shoris wife," later known as "Jane," and has been a significant influence on all subsequent accounts. The woman More describes deserves recognition for her good deeds at least as much as men who are famous for their evil ones. Her power, moreover, stems as much from Edward's inadequate self-control as from her own. Because Jane Shore's story serves a purpose, More emphasizes and even rather glamorizes it. Although Shore's victimization at the hands of Richard in More's account serves as an illustration of the latter's tyranny, her power functions as a symptom of the troubled nature of Edward's kingship. Oddly enough, More turns out to have been more ironic than he knew or probably would have wished to be. The very intersection between sex and politics, personal desire and affairs of state, that functioned as his critique of the York dynasty, recurred with a vengeance in the 1530s when Henry VIII set aside his wife to make his mistress Queen, changing the course of English history, and making Sir Thomas a martyr.

Notes

1   Perhaps genetically derived from Charles VI of France, his grandfather (Ross, *Wars* 24–5).

2   Richard was the descendant of John of Gaunt from his *first* marriage, and thus had more claim to authority than the Beaufort relatives. The Beauforts had their day in the end, however.

3   Rymer's *Foedera* quotes Richard's proclamation indicting Dorset, the queen's son by her first marriage, with having corrupted numerous "maids, widows, and wives" and in particular having lived in adultery with "The Wife of Shore." As with the Hastings' association, however, the accusation may have been more opportunistic than factual ("Unfortunate Royal Mistresses" 74).

4   "They tended to see the whole of 15th-century English history as a drama directed by God. The first Lancastrian king, Henry IV, had sinned by his unrighteousness in deposing Richard II. Eventually his sins were visited on the third generation of his family in the person of Henry VI, who was brought down, in a welter of blood, by the agents of divine retribution, the House of York. The Yorkists were themselves sinful, and reached a climax of wickedness in Richard III. Divine justice intervened again, and this time the saviour of England was Henry VII, whose marriage to Princess Elizabeth of York united the warring Houses, and made possible the triumphant reign of Henry VIII" (Ross, *Wars* 7).

5   See, for example, Strohm, chapter 5.

Chapter 2

Fatal Attractions: or, Jane Shore and the Popular Traditions

More's *Richard III*, dated c. 1514, is, according to James L. Harner, "the basis, directly or indirectly, for all later treatments of the story" ("Jane Shore in Literature" 496). By the time the next published treatment appeared, however, the story was substantially altered. Nevertheless, the tension between female sexuality and political power had, if anything, intensified. This is hardly surprising. Henry VIII's divorce and consequent break with the Church of Rome brought about radical realignments of power relations in England. To make matters even worse, the natural order of things seemed to have turned upside-down in the 16th century when, in quick succession, the monarchies of Scotland, England and France fell into the hands of—women.

The pain was particularly acute in England where, after the short reign of Henry VIII's only son, his daughter Mary (by the first wife so momentously cast aside) came to the throne and immediately threw the kingdom into turmoil by returning England to the control of Rome, and by making a stunningly unpopular marriage to Philip of Spain, to whom she would possibly have surrendered her kingdom, had she not been thwarted by her Council. After a (thankfully) brief five years, she was succeeded by her half-sister Elizabeth (daughter of the mistress who replaced Mary's mother as Queen). Although her legitimacy was never accepted by her Catholic enemies, who plotted time and again to depose her, Elizabeth was much more to her subjects' tastes, being Protestant. But she was still a woman, and for the next twenty-five years her sexual identity was a matter of grave national concern. The great fear was that Elizabeth might also be swayed by her female nature to make an imprudent match, delivering power into the hands of an unsuitable husband.

Her Council soon found that they had quite another problem on their hands: Elizabeth encouraged suitors, but refused all of them. While Mary's transgression had been understandable, in that of *course* a woman would defer to her husband, Elizabeth's was mystifying, in that she wouldn't have one at all. Her choice in the end was politically quite astute: her rebellion against social/sexual norms dismayed her people, but at the same time safeguarded them from "pillow talk" intervention.

Elizabeth's refusal to conform to social/sexual norms, however, also placed her in a kind of harlot/heroine bind: Unmarried, she necessarily constituted a very valuable prize *and* a focal point of lurid gossip. Her name was coupled scandalously with those of several men in her lifetime, notably the Earl of Leicester's, and her enemies pointedly scoffed at her claims to "virginity." Nevertheless, even they had to acknowledge and admire her shrewdness and political dexterity. The powerful/sexual woman paradox was, and is, very much at work in re-presentations of Elizabeth, past and present.[1]

Thomas Churchyard's "Howe Shores Wife, Edwarde the Fowerths Concubine, Was by King Richarde Despoyled of All Her Goodes, and Forced to Do Open Penance" appeared in *A Mirror For Magistrates* in 1563, five years into the reign of this complex monarch. While "politically correct" in its adherence to the Tudor party line vilifying all things York, critique of female rule could be tricky. The poet nevertheless takes this on, while developing several themes which add to the political anecdote elements of romantic tragedy and moral exemplum; More's Shore lacks pathos; Churchyard's has it in full measure. Clearly a strong popular tradition contributed to the story, and did as much or more to shape subsequent representations as Sir Thomas More's account.

The speaker in the poem is Shore's wife herself; turning the story into a first-person narrative instantly personalizes it to the reader, and there is a sense of urgency about "Howe Shores Wife ..." which furthers Churchyard's didactic purpose. Like More, Churchyard was a Tudor writer and took the Tudor party line on Richard III. By its title, one might think that Richard was the focus of the poem. However, like More, Churchyard is intrigued enough about Shore to explore even more fully Shore's background and feelings.

Churchyard tackles right away his task of presenting a heroine who is also a harlot; a victim who, in a sense, "deserves" punishment: a figure both sinned against and sinning. Jane Shore neatly sums up her position:

> The maiestie that kynges to people bear,
> The stately porte, the awful chere they show,
> Doth make the mean to shrynke and couche for feare,
> Like as the hound, that doth his maister know:
> What then, since I was made unto the bowe:
> There is no cloke, can serve to hyde my fault,
> For I agreed the fort he should assaulte. (78–84)

Churchyard seems to mitigate the hint of criticism toward royalty with Shore's assumption of primary fault. In the following stanza the kings's power over her takes on "naturally" irresistible proportions:

> The Egles force, subdues eche byrde that flyes,
> What mettal may resist the flaming fyre?
> Doth not the sonne, dasill the clearest eyes,
> And melt the ise, and make the frost retire?
> Who can withstand a puissaunt kynges desyre?
> The stiffest stones are perced through with tooles,
> The wisest are with princes made but fooles. (85–91)

Such psychological gymnastics are common to many of the 16th- to 18th-century representations of Jane Shore. Yes, I am at fault, she seems to say, but it was my unavoidable fate. This is a not unfamiliar misogynistic move in which the female sins by following her nature, is sinful, in fact, simply because she is female. Esther Yael Beith-Halahmi, on the other hand, claims that Churchyard's Shore stacks the deck, in a manner of speaking, in her own favor with her self-presentation:

> The self-castigations of the heroine, which add to Jane's qualities that of frankness, are almost always modified by the positive statements which precede or follow them. (86)

Beith-Halahmi adds that Shore's lines of self-praise outnumber those of self-denigration (85–6). She calls Shore's "weakness … part of the attractiveness of Churchyard's heroine" (73). She also, in passing, criticizes Churchyard's Edward, citing Castiglione's attribution of a beautiful woman's unchastity to her seducer (75–6). Beith Halahmi's study identifies Jane Shore primarily as an individual caught up in a personal passion. A woman, therefore constitutionally weak, she is also a subject bound to obedience. Add to this forced marriage, and the sum is extenuation, though not justification, of her transgression. Beith Halahmi's primary task seems to be to unearth Churchyard's sympathy for Shore rather than any broader political theme. Like More, however, Churchyard is interested in the political ramifications of the story; this is, after all, a Mirror for Magistrates as well as for parents and husbands.

While Churchyard's Shore certainly acknowledges guilt and responsibility, she also implicates external causes: her beauty, and forced marriage. Nature is called to task for clothing her in its "tapestrie" (100). But Churchyard (and/or the tradition upon which he is drawing) has come a long way from More's cryptic note that Shore might have been married "to sone;" we are invited to join Shore in condemnation of her "frends:"

> Before my time my youth they did abuse:
> In maryage, a prentyse was I bound,
> When that meere love I knewe not howe to use. (106–9)

The "prentyse" reference reminds us that Shore's husband was a man of business. By comparing marriage to apprenticeship, moreover, Churchyard degrades a relationship meant for spiritual and personal renewal by imposing upon it a purchase-sale aura.

Harner proposes that "meere" love has explicitly sexual connotations ("Churchyard's 'Shore's Wife'" 11–12); if so, the marriage begins to take on the aspect of a rape. Churchyard assigns no motive to the "frends" for marrying her off; subsequent treatments further elaborated on the theme and came up with various explanations. But while Shore reiterates that the fault is hers, Churchyard rams home his belief in the forced marriage's accountability:

> Note wel what stryfe this forced maryage makes,
> What loathed lyves do come where love doth lacke,
> What scratting bryers do growe upon such brakes,
> What common weales by it are brought to wracke,
> What heavy loade is put on paceintes backe,
> What straunge delyghts this braunch of vice doth brede
> And mark what graine sprynges out of such a seede. (120–26)

Forced marriage here, however, is more than an extenuation for adultery. It also has political consequences in the "wracke" of "common weales." The reference is reminiscent of contemporary treatises regarding the relationship between the domestic sphere—"a little commonwealth" (Gouge 18)—and the increasingly popular notion of a child's right of veto in the matter of choosing his or her partner. It also reminds us that there is more at stake here than one woman's chastity; the personal is political, and a king at the mercy of his libido posed a threat to the "common weale."

Three subsequent stanzas, in particular, elaborate on Shore's power in no uncertain terms:

> I never iard, in tune was every stryng,
> I tempered so my tounge to please his eare,
> That what I sayd was currant every where.

I ioynde my talke, my gestures, and my grace
In wittie frames that long might last and stand,
So that I brought the kyng in such a case,
That to his death I was his chiefest hand.
I governed him that ruled all this land:
I bare the sword though he did weare the crowne,
I strake the stroke that threwe the mightye downe.

    Yf iustice sayd that iudgement was but death,
With my sweete wordes I could the kyng perswade,
And make him pause and take therein a breath,
Tyl I wyth suyte the fawtors peace had made:
I knewe what waye to use him i his trade,
I had the arte to make the Lyon meeke,
There was no poynt wherein I was to seeke. (166–81, emphasis mine)

After claiming herself a weak woman powerless against the attractions and authority of a king, Shore now presents herself as the king's governor. It is a romantic concept, one picked up by many later accounts uncritically, but in the context of the period this declaration comprises a substantial critique of Edward. Indeed, Edward had already been criticized for up and marrying the penniless widow Elizabeth Woodville while negotiations were taking place for his marriage with the French princess. Further, the king had annoyed many of the nobility by exalting his wife's kin socially and giving them prominent positions due to members of older families. In the more politically outspoken 17th century, Charles I would be criticized for his excessive "uxoriousness;" although less public discourse emerged about Edward's similar vulnerability to the female principle, the potential political impact of his personal sexual escapades was not lost upon his councilors and some inhabitants of the city, who expressed their concern.

In a nutshell, a king should not be governed by any woman, certainly not by his mistress. In wielding the power she claims, Jane Shore indicts Edward of unkingly behavior. Kings were to be strong and firm and just; a king susceptible to "the arte to make the Lyon meeke" became a liability. The "Lyon" has no business being "meeke." In Churchyard, perhaps, is the most explicit commentary on Jane Shore's political influence as potentially dangerous. It matters not that she used it for good; she should not have had it at all.

Churchyard's primary target, like More's, is undoubtedly Richard III. But Jane Shore represents an opportunity to remind the reader that the whole Plantagenet dynasty was tainted and unfit for rule. In particular, the language Churchyard uses—the "natural" metaphors for Shore's seduction and the clearly political ones for her influence—paints a picture of a kingdom held hostage by the female principle—emotion, sexuality, and carnal instinct. It was bad enough that Edward's legal wife unduly influenced him; a mistress's influence was even more pernicious.

Also like More, however, Churchyard cannot restrain a certain admiration for Shore. We are meant to see the arrangement as injurious to the "common weale" by its very existence, but, thanks to Shore, not in its practice:

> To purchase prayse and winne the peoples zeale,
> Yea rather bent of kinde to do some good,
> I ever did upholde the common weale,
> I had delyght to save the gylteles bloud:
> Eche suters cause when that I understoode,
> I did preferre as it had bene mine owne,
> And helpt them up, that might have been oerthrowne.
>
> My power was prest to ryght the poore mans wrong,
> My handes were free to geve where nede requyred,
> To watche for grace I never thought it long,
> To do men good I nede not by desyred.
> Nor yet with gyftes my hart was never hyred. (197-208)

Shore, Churchyard makes clear, used her influence to "upholde the common weale," and prefer suitors' causes rather than her own. Like More, Churchyard admires Shore for her advocacy. Nevertheless, he has made us aware that Shore's individual integrity is an exception that proves the rule that a king governed by his sexual partner is a liability to the "common weale."

Such influence as Shore's is, in addition, highly vulnerable. Churchyard prepares us for the heroine's fall with a fairly standard commentary on fortune and ambition:

> What steppes of stryef belonge to highe estate?
> The clymynge up is doubtfull to undure,
> The seate it selfe doth purchase privie hate,
> And honours fame is fyckle and unsure,
> And all she brynges, is floures that be umpure:
> Which fall as fast as they do sprout and spring,
> And cannot last they are so vayne a thing. (225–31)

Merchants' wives are not entitled to "highe estate," regardless of how they use it, though they may acquire it temporarily. Such "fame" is brief and unstable. Unlike the narratives of queenly intervention on behalf of worthy suitors or those unfortunate enough to offend the king, Shore's advocacy, while admirable, does not fall into the same category of the interventions so celebrated by authors like Froissart and le Bel (Strohm 102).[2] Nor does it pay off, ultimately, with advocacy on *her* behalf on the part of those she has served. With twenty-twenty hindsight, Shore's wife laments her fall from grace to disgrace at the hands of the Protector:

> To such mischiefe this Tyrantes heart was bent.
> To God, ne man, he never stoode in awe,
> For in his wrath he made his wyll a lawe. (299–301)

The language of this passage further foregrounds the political implications of this personal tragedy. Churchyard stresses the word "tyrant," a common epithet for Richard in the 16th century, and a loaded term in the political thought of Early Modern England. A ruler swayed by wrath was just as bad as, if not worse than one swayed by sexuality, and Churchyard's audience would have seen the conflation of "wyll" and "lawe" as a direct threat to the "common weale." This passage also reminds us, however, of Shore's earlier appeal for understanding in the case of her adultery: "Who can withstand a puissant kings desyre?" (89). How great a difference is there, in fact, between a "tyrant" who makes his will law, and a king who places himself above social restraints and seduces another man's wife.

Deprived of her goods and abandoned to her fate in the streets, Shore's wife admonishes her readers:

> Thus long I lyved all weary of my life,
> Tyl death approcht and rid me from that woe:
> Example take by me both maide and wyfe,
> Beware, take heede, fall not to follie so,
> A myrrour make of my great overthrowe:
> Defye this world, and all his wanton wayes,
> Beware by me, that spent so yll her dayes. (386–92)

Churchyard elaborates on More's comment that good deeds are sooner forgotten than bad and asserts that Shore is driven into the street with no one to take "remorse" on her. He describes the contrast between her past grandeur and her current misery. Despite her assertion at the end of the poem that she is a negative example, Churchyard's Shore commands sympathy. Her adultery emerges as an unfortunate folly as against her "frends'" hard-heartedness,

Edward's weakness, and Richard's tyranny. As such a victim, she is clearly more appealing to Churchyard than as her king's governor. Powerless, she is safe to admire.

Churchyard's primary concern here is clearly the "common weale" rather than an individual woman's adultery. As the title, *A Mirror For Magistrates* implies, the poems collected in that volume are aimed at statesmen, not wayward merchants' wives. Her story is romantic and appealing, but Shore's advice to "Defye this world, and all his wanton wayes" is as much an admonition to kings as it is to "maide and wyfe." The state is only served when all its members, king and subject alike, respect the common weale and its legal and moral restrictions. Shore's wife succumbs to female frailty; Churchyard implies that this was inevitable. A king, however, should know better and be stronger.

In "Shore's Wife" Thomas Churchyard concentrates on the potential threat to the common weale posed by the power wielded by a king's mistress. He is careful, however, to exonerate this mistress of any specific wrongdoing beyond her adultery. The threat proceeds from the king's vulnerability to such a woman, not from the woman herself. Nevertheless, he acknowledges the powerful nature of female sexuality even as he warns against it. There is nothing subtle about his acknowledgement that Jane Shore was a politically influential personality. Such influence was problematic in contemporary political thought, however, and representing it required tact. Churchyard's poem is a courtier's poem; it does not question the integrity of royalty in general, or the social hierarchy (as he might, given Shore's commoner status). Instead, it represents social threat posed by persons who improperly wield their power, such as the "frends" and King Richard. Their abuse of power puts the common weale in jeopardy on both the domestic and political levels. Jane Shore's beneficial use of her power, however illegitimately acquired, mitigates her fault, but she ought not to have been accorded that power in the first place.

It is important to note that both More's and Churchyard's accounts of the woman we have come to know as Jane Shore identified the character simply as "Shore's wife." This appellation persisted in several poems dated in the 1590s. Thomas Deloney's "A New Sonnet, Conteining the Lamentation of Shore's Wife" (1593) and "The Wofull Lamentation of Mistris Jane Shore" (1597) are both ballads, suggesting their roots in popular culture. It is the latter text, however, that identifies her as "Jane."[3] The ballads' primary concern is domestic, not political, but they add some biographical and psychological details that would color many subsequent accounts. They reflect a less intellectual, more visceral distrust of female sexuality, as well as an increased pride in the distinct social identity, and upright ethos, of the merchant class.

Thomas Deloney's "A New Sonnet" appeared in a collection entitled *The Garland of Good Will* as "The Lamentation of Shore's Wife," to be sung, according to the note above the text, to the tune of "The Hunt is Up." Shore introduces herself abruptly:

> Shore's wife I am,
> So known by name;
> And at the Flower-de-Luce, in Cheapside, was my dwelling;
> The only daughter of a wealthy merchant-man,
> Against whose counsel I was evermore rebelling. (6-10)

More significant here than the Cheapside address (a well-known mercantile neighborhood of London) is the characterization of the merchant's daughter as rebellious. This is a significant offense since rebellion against a father's will was a direct challenge to the social order on the domestic level. And since the father as head of the household bore an analogous relationship to the king as head of the state (Smith 42, Whately 16), filial rebellion amounted to a kind of treason. By identifying Shore's wife as a rebellious daughter, Deloney's poem posits a psychology that would account for her subsequent rebellion against her husband, to whom she would be similarly subject. While this fleshes out the character it also tends to diminish her, reduce her in the hearer's mind to a wayward child rather than an active adult.

Having taken the trouble to psychologize her childhood, Deloney disposes peremptorily of her adultery:

> The king commanded, and I straight obey'd;
> For his chiefest jewell he did repute me. (19–20)

Note here again the absence of agency; Deloney's Shore casually tosses off her seduction as *droit de seignieur*; such a move mitigates criticism of Edward, and since Shore herself has already been established as wayward her matter-of-factness comes off as rather coarse. There is no mention of love on either side; Edward acquires and shows her off as a prized possession, a "jewel." This objectification occurs in subsequent representations, notably Michael Drayton's, in which Edward himself uses "jewel" language to describe Mistress Shore. The objectification also, of course further diminishes her agency.

Shore's high life lasts less than a single stanza:

> Bravely was I train'd,
> Like a queen I reign'd,
> And poor men's suits by me were obtain'd,
> In all the court, to none was suche great resort,
> As unto me, though now in scorne I be disdain'd. (21–5)

Significantly, this Shore's wife reigns, but only like a queen; she is not the governor of a king. There is no mention of her influence over Edward, and her power is only queen*like*, not legitimate.

The rest of the poem, more than half, is devoted to Shore's downfall and sufferings. Richard emerges as a villain who "took away my goods against all law and right" (30), but most of the rest of the text is devoted to a before-and-after comparison of Shore's circumstances: she who had had dainty dishes now begged for bread from door to door; once clothed richly, she now wore rags; vermin attacked the body the king used to embrace; used to soft beds, her "bones" lay now on hard stones and dirty straw (41–55). The passages contrast her two phases of life rather as More contrasts her 1514 self with her prime, but the repetitive pattern gives the account a more moralistic, explicitly judgmental tone.

The final stanza confirms the moral intent of the ballad:

> Wherefore, fair ladies,
> With your sweet babies
> My grievous fall bear in your mind, and behold me:
> How strange a thing that the love of a king
> Should come to die under a stall, as I told ye. (56–60)

Shore's wife commends her plight to "fair ladies" who but for her negative example might fall into sin, who might even already be rebellious against their divinely ordained roles as wives and mothers. "Love" finally gets a mention here, not as a feeling, but as a synonym for "concubine," which rather devalues the word in comparison to the "good" behavior Shore advises.

Deloney's ballad, unlike More's narrative and Churchyard's poem, has no political agenda; it is neither an adjunct to the Tudor myth nor a "mirror for magistrates." Even Richard is a minor character, though Deloney does note that he dispossessed Shore's wife "against all law and right." The whole thrust of the ballad focuses on Shore's fall from grace, first spiritually, in her rebelliousness and adultery, and then materially. The latter stands clearly as a moral punishment for the former, nothing more. Shore's political influence in the ballad is nil; what power she has is subtly diminished with the language used to describe it.

The introduction to the "Wofull Lamentation of Jane Shore" (c. 1597) in *Percy's Reliques of Ancient English Poetry* begins, "Though so many vulgar errors have prevailed concerning this celebrated courtesan, no character in history has been more perfectly handed down to us" (259). Unaware, apparently, of the irony of this statement,[4] editor Thomas Percy then goes on to quote More and Michael Drayton (who describes Shore in detail from a painting that may or may not be of Shore), and quotes Richard III's letter to the bishop of London. It is ironic that Percy does not identify the "vulgar errors" that he cites, given that much of the "history" he recounts clearly stems from popular elaboration. Percy gives the full title of the ballad as "The woeful lamentation of Jane Shore, a goldsmith's wife in London, sometime king Edward IV. his concubine. To the tune of "Live with me," &c" (261).

From the title itself we can see that more biographical information has found its way into print. The ballad's didactic intent is easily identified in the refrain to every verse:

> Then maids and wives in time amend
> For love and beauty will have end.

We have here a pretty straightforward message, primarily a warning to attractive young women that "love and beauty" (a causal link?) do not last and that those who depend on those insubstantials face disappointment. This message is reinforced in the title cited by Harner ("Jane Shore in Literature" 497): "The Wofull Lamentation of Mistris Jane shore a Goldsmiths Wife of London, Sometimes K. Edwards Concubine, Who for Her Wanton Life Came to a Most Miserable End. Set Forth for an Example to All Lewd Women."

The ballad begins by invoking another famous mistress, Rosomonde, Henry II's concubine, reputedly poisoned by his queen, the jealous Eleanor of Aquitaine. And although the primary didactic purpose of the ballad is undoubtedly a warning to fair women, it takes up other vital issues as well, some familiar, some new. First is the issue of forced marriage. The "friends" of Churchyard's poem have been fleshed out here, or at least their motivation has:

> My parents they, for thirst of gaine,
> A husband for me did obtaine;
> And I, their pleasure to fulfille,
> Was forc'd to wedd against my wille. (9–12)

Deloney's protagonist introduced herself as rebellious; the "Lamentation's" Shore describes herself particularly as "wanton," and attributes her fall to lust. There is no eliding the sexuality of this Jane Shore:

> To Matthew Shore[5] I was a wife,
> Till lust brought ruine to my life;
> And then my life I lewdlye spent,
> Which makes my soul for to lament.
>   * * *
> I spred my plumes, as wantons doe,
> Some sweet and secret friende to wooe,
> Because chast love I did not finde
> Agreeing to my wanton minde. (13–16, 21–4)

Whereas Churchyard and Deloney both regard the forced marriage as in some degree responsible for Shore's downfall, the "Lamentation" glosses over that detail in four lines and creates an image of Shore as an adulteress just waiting to happen. She lives "lewdlye;" she behaves "as wantons doe;" her mind itself is "wanton." Her name comes to Edward's ear,

> Who came and lik'd, and love requir'd,
> But I made coye what he desir'd. (27–8)

Even her response to the king has a negative connotation. She does not resist because she is married; rather, she is "coye" and plays hard to get. There is no indication that she feels any attraction to Edward, although she is "beloved" by him, according to her friend Mistress Blague.

This is the first account in print to include Mistress Blague, sometimes identified as a lace-maker. She appears in many of the narratives that follow and she is usually drawn in accordance with her subsequent betrayal of Shore; that is, as a shrewd, worldly woman out to better herself through others. In this, as in other versions, she takes at least some of the rap for Jane's downfall:

> By her persuasions I was led
> For to defile my mariage-bed,
> And wronge my wedded husband Shore,
> Whom I had married yeares before. (33–6)

Yet the ballad is very quick to re-focus agency (and thus guilt) on Shore herself in the very next stanza:

In hearte and minde I did rejoyce,
That I had made so sweet a choice;
And therefore did my state resign
To be king Edward's concubine. (37–40)

Any note of remorse that might ring in lines 33–6 is quickly drowned out by the complacency of the following stanza. She admits she did "defile" her marriage-bed and "wronge" her husband, but nevertheless rejoices in heart and mind at her "sweet" choice. Unlike Churchyard's protagonist, the "Lamentation's" Shore seems to commit adultery quite cheerfully. She also abandons her "state," i.e., her proper station in life as a wife and a commoner.

This Jane Shore, then, is an essentially sexual woman (defined as "wanton"), with the possible extenuations of her transgression downplayed and her pleasure in it emphasized. This is a much less sympathetic character, and even more poetically appropriate as a negative example, than Deloney's protagonist. Moreover, the "Lamentation's" Edward is a powerful, attractive being, who appears blameless, even admirable. Shore states that her husband's bed, "though wrong'd by a king,/ His heart with deadlye griefe did sting" (53-4), as if it was rather in bad taste for the cuckold to take it so hard; after all, how many men get to be cuckolded by a king?

He could not live to see his name
Impair'd by my wanton shame;
Although a prince of peerless might
Did reape the pleasure of his right. (57–60)

The king's offense here is more or less neutralized by his "peerless might," leaving Jane Shore's "wanton shame" to bear the brunt of censure.

As for Shore's courtly influence, the "Lamentation" essentially de-politicizes it, and diminishes it as well. Certainly, the speaker boasts that she "knew the secrets of a king" (44). But her use and extent of her power seems fairly trivial:

When I was thus advanc'd on highe
Commanding Edward with mine eye,
For Mrs. Blague I in short space
Obtainede a livinge from his grace.

No friend I had but in short time
I made unto a promotion climbe. (45–50)

This is mere nepotism; there are no weighty suits or great displeasures. This Jane Shore behaves, rather, as other accounts accuse Elizabeth Woodville of behaving. But even Elizabeth's use of power was more politically significant than this: the queen specifically advanced her already aristocratic, though upstart, relatives to positions of high nobility and authority; she was at least partially responsible for the power struggle that arose at Edward's death between her own relations and Gloucester's and Lord Hastings' faction over the control of Edward V. The advancement of Jane Shore's "friends," by contrast, remains on the petty scale of the "livinge" she arranged for Mistress Blague.

Two stanzas later, Shore describes her generosity toward the needy:

> But yet a gentle minde I bore
> To helplesse people, that were poore;
> I still redrest the orphan's crye,
> And sav'd their lives condemned to dye.
>
> I still had ruth on widowes tears,
> I succour'd babes of tender years;
> And never looked for other gaine
> But love and thanks for all my paine. (65–72)

The humble-sounding nature of these doings restricts Jane Shore's advocacy to suitably "feminine" objects: widows, orphans, the helpless. Again the implication is that her scope of interest was reassuringly small and unlikely to make any big difference in court politics.

The remainder of the ballad chronicles Shore's degradation at the hands of Richard ("This tyrant") after Edward's death, never forgetting that the degradation is deserved by reason of the "sin/ That I so long had liv'd in" and the "lewd and wanton life/ That made a strumpet of a wife" (77–82). Even Richard's perfidy is glossed over in favor of the retributional tone.

The same kinds of contrasts between her former "state" and her poverty echo Deloney's ballad, with the addition of the reminder that even people who wished to help Jane Shore were forbidden by law to do so. Here another detail enters the story, subsequently to be repeated often: one man Shore aided in her days of prosperity does try to help her and is hanged for his pains.

Finally, we realize that the speaker has all along been a ghost when she announces

> Thus, weary of my life, at lengthe
> I yielded up my vital strength,

Within a ditch of loathsome scent,
Where carrion dogs did much frequent:

The which now since my dying daye,
Is Shoreditch call'd as writers saye;
Which is a witness of my sinne,
For being concubine to a king. (129–36)

The ballad ends with a series of admonitions to wives and husbands:

You wanton wives, that fall to lust,
Be you assur'd that God is just:
Whoredome shall not escape his hand,
Nor pride unpunish'd in this land.

If God to me such shame did bring
That yielded only to a king,
How shall they scape that daily run
To practice sin with every one?

You husbands, match not but for love,
Lest some disliking after prove:
Women, be warn'd when you are wives,
What plagues are due to sinful lives:
  Then, maids and wives, in time amend,
  For love and beauty will have end. (137–48)

Although the balance of these last stanzas targets wives and warns them against lust, husbands also come in for a small share of advice in the warning to "match not but for love," a line which rather belatedly suggests to us that Matthew Shore was not exempt from his wife's parents' "thirst of gaine."

Nevertheless, the ballad's primary agenda is a warning to women against lust, a warning by example of a woman who yielded "only" to a king and still bore God's harsh punishment. This is not just a warning to wives to avoid seductive kings; it posits a danger far closer to home and much less improbable. The warning is clear: if Jane Shore suffered so much for having yielded to a king, how much more ought a woman to suffer who cuckolds her husband with just anybody?

Balladry is an oral form: the simple format and rhyme scheme, coupled with a popular or catchy new tune, facilitate easy transmission of the story and yet allow for some flexibility in the details. It is impossible to say how much

the published versions of the above ballads differ from their originals—we
are once again at the mercy of the "Post Office" phenomenon—but it is clear
that they reflect the concerns of their audience. As we saw in Churchyard's
poem, however, more literary forms of story-telling also reflect the concerns
of their audience. *The Mirror For Magistrates* is just that, a series of exempla
against which those in power ought to assess themselves. The popular ballads
concern themselves with issues facing real people: social climbing, the
potential for adultery in a crowded and mercantile city, material gain over
parental responsibility, the nature of marriage.

Whereas the ballads set forth the story of an individual as a moral exemplum,
there appears another form concerned with beauty and romance, calculated
to arouse the sensibilities. While the popular ballads combine entertainment
with moral advice, these more "courtly" poems appeal to the emotions without
great effort to dictate personal sexual behavior or warn against "wracke" of the
"common weale." Two poets of the 1590s wrote in this style, Anthony Chute
and Michael Drayton. Their "takes" on Jane Shore offer another perspective
and additional biographical speculation.

Writing of Chute's "Bewtie Dishonoured, Written under the Title of Shores
Wife" (1593), Beith-Halahmi claims that "all other elements are subservient
to the central glorification of beauty" (128). The poem begins with a rather
surprising invocation:

> Sigh, sad musde accents, of my funerall verse,
> In lamentable grones, (wrought from true pietie)
> Sing you the wept song, on her wronged hearce,
> In gratefull obsequie to her mortall deitie:
> Sighe: O sing Actuallie the bewtie pained,
> With bewties wonder honorablie stained. (1–6)

"Deitie" is hardly a word we have associated, up to now, with Jane Shore.[6] And
what about the oxymoron "honorablie stained?" While the ballads get down
to the business of story-telling quite promptly, Chute's poem goes on in this
vein for several stanzas, invoking pity, elegies, and recognition of beauties of
the past. Chute appears to mourn that "now she seems as if she had bin never,/
Whom even eternitie said should live forever" (17–18). Chute attributes this
disappearance to the forgetfulness of his contemporaries. Indeed, he complains,
the story is only remembered now by those who want to denigrate beauty:
"The high-musde period of the storie reader ... Omits her fortune, to her fates
arreader,/ (Precisely censuring bewtie by her error)/ So she that even the fairest

she surmounted,/ Now of the fairest, is the fowlest counted" (19–24). These "precise" critics posit an inevitable association between beauty and error.[7]

Beith-Halahmi's assessment of "Bewtie Dishonored" as a hymn to beauty seems essentially correct. Beauty is, as she claims, the central element around which Chute organized his poem. Even Richard cannot remain unmoved by it; Beith-Halahmi asserts that lust (provoked by Shore's beauty) evokes in Richard a desire to "ravish" his late brother's mistress (137). Richard's sputtering, almost inarticulate rage certainly invites such an interpretation, as does the language used to describe it: Chute compares Richard to "an angerie Bull incenst with yre…Impatient, madd, wanting his lustes desire" (1093, 1095); having Shore stripped and turned into the street seems only to stir up his frenzy further:

> So unappeas'd, unquyet, mad and yrefull
> Rages th'insatiate furie of his will,
> And in his looke, fierce, wan, and pale, and dyrefull
> He seem's impatient, moodie, madded, still,
> And not content with this disgrace to greeve me
> He sayes that all shall dye (that dare relieve me). (1099–104)

Like Churchyard's, Chute's Richard III also "Acte[s] all thinges at his will: for will was law" (1032).

As in "The Woefull Lamentation," Jane Shore wields only stereotypically feminine power in this poem; her political influence is elided completely. When Shore realized the king admires her,

> My brows recusancie gan tyrannise,
> And of my king exact a tribute dutie,
> And if he proffered love, I would forsake it,
> For woemen first say no, and then they take it. (639–42)

The cynicism Shore reveals as she plays hard to get coincides with the "coyness" attributed to her in the "Woefull Lamentation." But the John Donne-esqe bitterness of the last line goes further. This is a broad misogynistic comment on all "woemen" (even the spelling, whether Chute's own or his editor's, is condemnatory). This is clearly more than "just" a celebration of beauty.

Edward's fault, if any, is completely elided here:

> But he that could command thee, made thee sin,
> Yet that is no priviledge, no sheeld to thee:

> Now thou thy selfe hast drowned thy selfe therein.
> Thou art defam'd thy selfe, and so is hee (709–12)

Shore's responsibility for defamation, at first, applies not only to her, but also to her seducer. Yet Chute follows this up with something new:

> And though that kings commands have wonders wrought
> Yet kings commands could never hinder thought. (713–14)

Chute here articulates the growing belief in the limitations of kingship: subjects are bound to obey, but the sovereign's commands must be just. Furthermore, each subject's conscience is her own; that the king's commands "could never hinder thought" reminds us of the scope Chute's Puritan (and other) contemporaries were beginning to extend to conscience. This tends to add to Jane Shore's fault, of course: the possession of conscience entails the responsibility to obey it, and not the king, if what he commands is wrong.[8]

Jane Shore's influence on the political level does not apparently concern Chute except in that he takes some pains to establish its limits:

> And though my life had staine, yet this did mend it,
> That I was sorrie such an one to be,
> And this was commendably praysd in me,
> That Sutor wrongs my selfe to right would bring,
> If right might be procured from the king. (733–8)

The "if" and "might" of the last line make it clear that the king is still very much in control and deciding for himself what suits to reward. Furthermore, like the ballads' Shore, Chute's seems primarily to employ her influence in sensual pleasure, not in the weighty matters More alleges:

> And now so deem'd so highly was I prysed,
> No honor was too good, too great for mee,
> I could commaund what ever thought devised,
> Delight to sence, or ioyes to mynde to bee:
> And whilst I sat seated alone so highe,
> The king could but command and so could I. (739–44)

Her pleasures are all of sense and mind, and although she is seated "so highe," she is also "prysed," i.e., objectified.

Chute's Jane Shore also lacks the humility found in the ballads' Shores. The latter are concerned for the people who endanger themselves to help her; the former finds the mere notion of begging so distasteful that she would rather starve (1111–34). She expires at a leisurely pace, "A witherd lilly" (1160), pale as crystal (1201), mortal in her body, immortal in her fame:

> Yet would they part the remnant of her being
> Her body went to death; her fame to life.
> Thus life, and death, in unitie agreeing,
> Dated the tenor of their sondrie strife,
> Death vow'd her body should be eyed never,
> Yet life hath vow'd her fame should live for ever. (1207–12)

Her fame, however, rests solely on her beauty, something of a paradox since that beauty is responsible for her body's (the vehicle of that beauty) ultimate disappearance. She is in fact the best of all beauties: one that lives on in imagination, or "fame;" she can never disappoint because she is not "real." Thus Chute ultimately deprives Jane Shore of independent being, consigning her to his own and his readers' imaginations.

Chute's poem is, throughout, more self-consciously "literary" than the ballads, employing extended metaphor and digressing often for contemplation. These things reflect the poem's reading audience's interest in meaning and truth not established by plot alone. This audience is not, however, as interested in political meaning as Churchyard's; the poem is largely devoid of commentary on royalty or statecraft. Even Richard III's motivation is reduced to a lust-crazed frenzy. Moreover, there is no "moral" lesson articulated in the poem as in the ballads, and the implicit criticism of Edward is absent. It would be a mistake, however, to say that "popular" and "sophisticated" audiences invariably took a different view of the affair, for Churchyard's poem is nothing if not "sophisticated" and it articulates both Shore's influence and criticism of Edward.

On an entirely different level are Michael Drayton's two poems, "Edward the Fourth to Mistres Shore" and "The Epistle of Mistres Shore to King Edward the Fourth," which appear in a series of Historicall Epistles (1597) that deal mostly with "world-historical events" rather than pure romance. Pure romance these two poems are, however, and unique among the texts considered in this study because we are invited to imagine the courtship only. Drayton is well aware, as his subsequent notes indicate, that the relationship he depicts is an "unlawfull" and therefore indecorous subject for poetry, historical or otherwise (this comment is quite clearly tongue-in-cheek, since one can name any number of great works written about "unlawfull" relationships). At any rate, he neatly solves this "problem" by leaving us with a pre-fall Jane Shore; she and the king exchange beautiful reparteés without carrying them through to their conclusion.

Richard does not appear at all in these poems; clearly Drayton had no interest in contributing to the Tudor propaganda against Richard. Nevertheless, his Edward is reduced to a king overcome with love for a rare, but plebian, beauty. Not that Mistress Shore seems plebian in her epistle; she is as clever with language and as refined as her royal lover. Indeed, these epistles have a dictinctly Petrarchan feel all the way through. Edward metaphorically greets Shore in her husband's shop as a "Jewell" for which "Would not my Treasure serve, my Crowne should goe" ("Edward the Fourth" 45), and which "My Kingly Scepter onely should redeeme" (49). Edward launches into a panegyric so extravagantly Petrarchan it is almost parodic:

> I smile to thinke, how fond th'italians are,
> To judge their articifiall Gardens rare;
> When London in thy Cheekes can shew them heere
> Roses and Lillies growing all the yeere:
> The Portugall, that onely hopes to win,
> By bringing Stones from farthest India in;
> When happie SHORE can bring them forth a Girle,
> Whose Lips be Rubies, and her Teeth be Pearle. (53–60)

He goes on to criticize Shore's husband for valuing gold and jewels and not seeing how superior she is to all of them (71 ff), and wonders that her husband cannot adequately prize the beauty that must make every man who comes into the shop love her. Beauty, he declares, is the common desire of all men, enjoyed by all sorts and conditions except those for whom it is "too deare."

> So much is Beautie pleasing unto all,
> That Prince and Pesant equally doth call;
> Nor never yet did any Man despise it,
> Except too deare, and that he could not prize it. (119–22)

Edward is either accusing Master Shore of not recognizing the prize he has, or he is lamenting that the prize is "too deare" to be won. A woman, the possession of whom has already been valued at a king's treasure, crown, and scepter, might indeed be "too deare," as the final lines of the first poem conclude,

Meane while, receive that Warrant by these Lines,
Which Princely Rule and Sov'raigntie resignes;
Till when, these Papers, by their Lords command,
By me shall kisse they sweet and daintie Hand. (167–70)

Drayton's Edward is charming, but not very kingly except in the elegance of his speech. He certainly has no business resigning "Princely Rule and Sov'raigntie"! One may argue that these are all merely figures of speech, and not meant to reflect Drayton's opinion of Edward. However, the poet also left less subtle hints of this opinion.

Not content with imagining the courtship between Edward IV and Mistress Shore, Drayton provides the reader with historical "annotations," although, as he admits, "the unlawfull nature" of their "Affection ministreth small occasions of Historicall Notes" (252). Drayton tells the reader that King Edward "was by nature very Chivalrous, and very Amorous, applying his sweet and amiable Aspect to attaine his wanton Appetite the rather," recounting an episode when the king's nature supposedly affected international diplomacy. Drayton concludes his description ominously:

Edward's intemperate desires, with which he was wholly overcome, how tragically they in his Off-spring were punished, is universally knowne. A Mirrour, representing thier Over-sight, that rather leave their Children what to possess, then what to imitate. (252)

This account goes so far as to suggest that Edward, not Richard, bears ultimate moral responsibility for the Princes' deaths. A king certainly ought not to be "overcome" by "intemperate desires." Drayton thus sharpens the "Mirrour" image proposed by Churchyard.

In so many accounts of Edward, Richard, and Jane Shore, Richard is such an easy target that we can miss subtle criticisms of Edward like More's, Churchyard's, and Drayton's. Ricardian apologists notwithstanding, history has tended to "throw the book" (as Thomas B. Costain puts it) at Richard and not really bother with the rest of the cast. Although Drayton refers to Richard as a "tyrant," he rationalizes Richard's cruelty to Shore as political spin.

What her father's name was, or where she was borne, is not certainly knowne: but Shore, a yong man of right goodly person, wealth, and behaviour, abandoned her bed, after the King had made her his Concubine. Richard the third causing her to doe open penance in Pauls Church-yard, commanded that no man should relieve her, which the tyrant did not so much for his hatred to sinne, but that by making his brothers life odious, he might cover his horrible treasons the more cunningly. (259)

Richard might have been a "tyrant," but Drayton rather confirms that Edward's life was, if not "odious," at least irresponsible.

Drayton's Edward does make rather a fool of himself, a Petrarchan lover who does not know what is due to his position and responsibilities. Drayton may also be invoking another Petrarchan lover, Sir Philip Sidney's Astrophil in sonnet #75:

> Of all the Kings that euer here did raigne,
> *Edward*, nam'd fourth, as first in praise I name
> Not for his faire outside, nor well-lin'd braine,
> Although lesse gifts impe feathers oft on fame
> Nor that he could, young-wise, wise-valiant, frame
> His sires reuenge, ioyn'd with a kingdomes gaine;
> And gain'd by *Mars*, could yet mad *Mars* so tame,
> That balance weigh'd, what sword did late obtaine
> Nor that he made the floure-de-luce so 'fraid,
> (Though strongly hedg'd) of bloudy lyons pawes,
> That wittie Lewes to him a tribute paid:
> Nor this, nor that, nor any such small cause;
> But only for this worthy King durst proue
> To lose his crowne, rather than faile his loue.[9]

The first passage of Drayton's "annotations" seems to recall this sonnet specifically:

> This Epistle of Edward to Mistres Shore, and of her to him, being of unlawfull Affection, ministreth small occasion of Historicall Notes; for had he mentioned the many Battels betweixt the Lancastrian Faction and him, or other Warlike Dangers, it had beene more like to Plautus boasting Souldier, then a Kingly Courtier. (252)

Plautus, of course, was a comic playwright, and *the miles gloriosus* he invokes is a stock figure of comedy. Indeed, so is the Petrarchan lover. However, the blatant allusion to the Petrarchan sonnet again suggests a *political* context. The "Kingly Courtiers" who wrote such sonnets were almost exclusively, according to Arthur Marotti, *not* kings, but courtier-supplicants to the aging Elizabeth, couching their political ambitions in the language of sexual desire (404). The role-reversal, here, of a king pleading for the favors of a merchant's wife, may reflect the emasculating effect of the (superior) man's dependence on the whim of the (inferior) woman for, not love, but for social and political advancement.[10]

But what about Jane Shore herself? Where is her voice, her personality, in this text? Drayton remarks that

> Her stature was meane, her haire of a darke yellow, her face round and full, her eye gray, delicate harmony being betwixt each parts proportion, and each proportions coulour, her bodie fat, white, and smooth, her countenance cheerfull, and like to her condition. (258)

The reference to Shore's "cheerfull" countenance, "like to her condition" is intriguing; this is not the portrait of a penitent, nor yet that of a woman caught between duty and desire. This is a pre-adultery Shore, frozen in mid-seduction, with all the glory of being loved by a king and none of the stigma of having succumbed to him. The first sixty-five lines of "Hers to Him" modestly respond to Edward's praise of her own beauty and echo Edward's belittlement of "beauties" in other lands. Only after this extended introduction does she refer to her personal situation. She admits to being "married when I was but yong,/ Before I knew what did to Love belong" (67-8), but declares herself innocent of any entanglement with another, though assailed by the "strong'st Batt'rie" (76). She wonders whether the king supposes "that I repuls'd the rest,/ To leave a King the conquest of my Brest,/ And have thus long preserv'd my selfe from all,/ To have a Monarch glory in my fall" (77-80). She follows up with the apparently unambiguous couplet, "Yet rather let me die the vildest death,/ Then live to draw that sinne-polluted breath" (81-2). However, without even a break, she continues,

> But our kind hearts, Mens Teares cannot abide,
> And we least angry oft, when most we chide.
> Too well know Men what our Creation made us,
> And Nature too well taught them to invade us:
> They know but too well how, what, when, and where,
> To write, to speake, to sue, and to forbeare,
> By signs, by sighes, by motions, and by teares,
> When Vowes should serve, when Oathes, when Smiles, when Prayers.
> (83–90)

Without missing a beat, Drayton's Shore seems to be setting up an excuse in advance similar to Churchyard's: it is women's nature that makes them err.

Unlike Churchyard, however, Drayton does not stop at female nature, but specifically and shrewdly implicates *men's* "natural" propensity to assault women's virtue and subsequently to hold the women alone responsible:

> And yet so shamelesse, when you tempt us thus,
> To lay the fault on Beautie and on us.
> Romes wanton Ovid did those Rules impart,
> O, that your Nature should be help'd with Art! (101–4)

In passing, it is interesting to note that Drayton bestows upon the mercer's wife's familiarity, or at least acquaintance, with the classics. The next two lines once more remind us of the larger issues at stake here:

> Who would have thought, a King that cares to raigne,
> Inforc'd by Love, so Poet-like should faine? (105–6)

The language of these two lines seems designed to sting. "A King that cares to raigne" suggests that this king is casual about his commitment. He is "Inforc'd" by love, disempowered by emotion. Finally, he's only "Poet-*like*," and feigning, at that; he's not even a real poet. How the mighty are fallen! But once again Shore reverses herself mid-repulse:

> But yet I know more then I meane to tell,
> (O would to God you knew it not too well!)
> That Women oft their most admirers rayse,
> Though publiquely not flatt'ring their own prayse. (105–8)

One cannot help concluding that Drayton's Shore seriously opens herself to the charge of being a tease, and rather calls into question the sincerity of her high-minded scorn in lines 77–80.

Drayton's Shore then continues with a new twist on the trials of her married life. She blames husbands who, having sated themselves with their wives' youth, now ignore and neglect them, finding their pleasure elsewhere with "Venus in a Bed of Downe" (128). At the same time, these husbands are jealous and paranoid, restricting their wives' "publique Walking, our loose Libertie" (134). Barring their wives from the theater both comic and tragic, husbands nevertheless "very hardly keepe us safe at home;/ And oft are touch'd with feare and inward griefe,/ Knowing rich Prizes soonest tempt a Thiefe" (144–6). The commodification evident in the first epistle is even less flattering when seen through the eyes of the commodified.

Here, Drayton is anachronistic. There were no public theaters to speak of, in late 15th-century London—and Shore speaks of "churlish Husbands" in the plural; Drayton is merely calling upon the stereotype of the Elizabethan merchant husband vulnerable to and terrified of cuckoldry (Woodbridge 174) to appeal to his contemporary audience.

The conclusion of Shore's "epistle" leaves no doubt as to the eventual outcome:

> Thus still we strive, yet overcome at length,
> For men want mercie, and poore women strength:
> Yet grant, that we could meaner men resist,
> When Kings once come, hey conquer as they list.
> Thou art the cause, Shore pleaseth not my sight,
> That his embraces give me no delight;
> Thou art the cause I to my selfe am strange,
> Thy comming is my Full, thy Set my Change.
> Long Winter nights be minutes, if thou heere,
> Short minutes, if thou absent, be a yeere.
> And thus by strength thou art become my fate,
> And mak'st me love even in the mid'st of hate. (157–68)

Interestingly, though Shore earlier gives ample and independent reasons for disliking her husband, she now attributes that dislike entirely to Edward. The final couplet is striking in two ways. First, Shore says that Edward has become her "fate," and then that she loves "in the mid'st of hate." Subtly, Drayton's Shore distances herself from agency in the inevitable adultery to follow. Earlier she compares women's lack of strength to men's lack of "mercie." No one can avoid her "fate," not even "The holi'st Nunne" (156). It remains to ask, at whom is the hate in the last line directed? Herself, her husband, or Edward? Is this the hint of moral struggle for which an apologist searches? Is it justification on the grounds of marital incompatibility? Or is it a subtle criticism of a king's abuse of power? Whatever the answer, the line tends to minimize Shore's active agency in the adultery to come; note that Edward "mak'st" her love.

To sum up, then, the 16th-century variations on the Jane Shore theme both develop the details of the legend itself and concern themselves with contemporary issues. While Churchyard and Drayton, in different ways, expand upon the potential *political* ramifications of a monarch's vulnerability to his libido hinted at in More, the story resonates with additional anxieties about beauty, marriage, ambition and female transgression. And the intersection of sexuality and royal power reflects and attempts to contain a tension that was inevitably very much on the minds of 16th-century writers. Ironically, while Jane Shore transgressed sexual norms by committing adultery, Queen Elizabeth transgressed them also: by remaining *faithful* to the only spouse she claimed she would ever take, her people. She would not, unlike Edward, allow anyone else to "bare the sword though [she] did weare the crowne" (Churchyard 174).

Drayton and the ballad-makers, finally, reveal a very different social context than More's, Churchyard's, and even Chute's. The added interest in Shore's origins, and the specific social sphere she abandons to become a king's mistress, testify to the increased importance of the London citizen, not just as a character in literature but as a consumer of it. The ballads in particular evoke a distinct ethos that proudly defines itself against courtly indulgence, while it simultaneously warns its members against the excesses of pride and greed associated with the aristocracy that are coming within their reach. Jane Shore's adultery is more than a betrayal of her husband, but also a transgression against the collective morality of those of her social position. Edward's "command" is no longer taken as a matter of course; Shore has to accept the responsibility for her action as the price of the autonomy increasingly asserted by the citizenry.

All of these texts, added on to More's, begin to establish a pretty comprehensive portrait of Mistress Shore. But late 16th-century London was the cradle of a new, dynamic form of popular culture which, it is argued, both shaped and reflected these changing social dynamics.[11] The Jane Shore story is inevitably part of the development of popular drama, in particular as it contributes to the emerging genre of domestic tragedy. And it is in domestic tragedy that the intersection between sexual and social transgression is most apparent.

Notes

[1]   Witness its extremely graphic re-presentation in the largely ahistorical film, *Elizabeth* (1998).

[2]   "Official ideologists like le Bel and Froissart, and a host of other chroniclers and petitioners and poets, joined enthusiastically in producing representations of queenly mediation, and no 14th-century queen could have failed to understand that mediatory activities would comprise a large part of her job description."

[3]   Even if her given name, Elizabeth, had not been forgotten, as is most probable, it would not do to have a harlot/heroine of the same name as the reigning monarch.

[4]   The *Reliques* were first published in 1885.

5   Jane Shore's husband's name alternates between "William" and "Matthew" in a majority of the texts in this study.

6   Yet Shakespeare uses the word to describe her, too in *Richard III*. See Chapter 3.

7   Are these, perhaps, the ballad-writers?

8   "Direct loyalty to God should bypass all mediators and mesne lords ... Archbishop Grindal warned Elizabeth that, though she was a mighty princess, yet, 'He that dwelleth in heaven is mightier'" (Hill 27).

9   Though the "love," here is obviously Elizabeth Woodville (Edward's marriage to her having precipitated Warwick's betrayal), the poem usefully backs up the argument that Tudor culture generally viewed Edward, not just Richard, as unfit to wear the crown, due to his mixed up priorities.

10   "... Bacon put his finger on the essence of Elizabethan politics: first, that to succeed at Court politicians have to pretend to be in love with the queen; secondly, that the conduct of the 'game' of courtship was Elizabeth's most effective tool of policy. For the dithering, prevarication and generally dismissive behaviour which was understood to be archetypal of the conventional 'mistress' provided Elizabeth with her weapons of political manipulation and manoeuvre" (Guy 3).

11   See Greenblatt 8.

Chapter 3

'Tis Pity She's a Whore: or, Jane Shore on the Boards

Arguably the most eclectic of the popular media in the 1590s was the public theater; all sorts and conditions of persons frequented the playhouses. Like balladry, drama did not depend on literacy for transmission, and almost all social status-levels found the price affordable. Despite some Puritans' attacks on the theater, its supporters defended the theater's exemplary value. Thomas Heywood, though himself of increasingly Puritan sympathies, roundly defended the stage against Puritan attack in his *Apology for Actors* (1612), and continued an active playwright into the 1630s.

Between 1593–99 three plays that touched on the Jane Shore story appeared on the popular stage. In the most famous of these, Shakespeare's *Richard III*, Shore doesn't even appear, but she is referenced in a manner that indicates Shakespeare accessed primarily the chronicle tradition of More. The anonymous *True Tragedie of Richard III* includes Jane Shore in the *dramatis personae*, and interestingly represents her as somewhat more cynical and knowing, as the ballad tradition would have her. In the end, it is Thomas *Heywood's King Edward the Fourth, Parts I and II*, which provides the most comprehensive and at the same time popularly-inspired representation of Jane Shore. While the first two plays (as their titles suggest) take their primary aim at Richard, Heywood's is more comprehensive, suggesting additional critique of Edward. Heywood's play, too, takes on the social tension between aristocrat and citizen in a new way, once more championing a new morality based on domestic affection and loyalty to one's own caste.

William Shakespeare, *Richard III*

As blasphemous as it may seem, we can quickly dispose of Shakespeare as a contributor to the Shore legend. She is mentioned in the play only in two scenes, the second of which more or less dramatizes the episode in More when the Protector accuses Hastings of conspiring with Shore and the Queen to wither his arm by means of witchcraft. Shakespeare is perfectly faithful

to More here, right down to Richard's request for strawberries from Bishop
Morton's garden. Very early in the play, however, Shore is the object of a
verbal pleasantry, from which one might get an impression that the King's
mistress was definitely a player in the affairs of the court.

In Act one, scene one Richard passes off Clarence's arrest on suspicion of
treason as the result of an intrigue on the part of "the Queen's kindred" who
have used Shore as a go-between to the King. This impression of her power
suits Richard very well, given that he is primarily responsible for his brother's
arrest. He also provides a commentary on Edward that makes explicit More's
veiled criticism:

> Why, this it is, when men are rul'd by women. (I.i.62)

Richard here may be referring primarily to the Queen; Clarence, however,
takes up the theme and introduces Shore:

> By heaven, I think there is no man secure
> But the Queen's kindred, and night-walking heralds
> That trudge between the King and Mistress Shore.

Richard takes back the ball and runs with it a little more, crediting Shore with
the recent release of Hastings:

> Humbly compaining to her deity
> Got my Lord Chamberlain his liberty.
> I tell you what, I think it is our way,
> If we will keep in favor with the King,
> To be her men and wear her livery.
> The jealous o'erworn widow and herself
> Since that our brother dubb'd them gentlewomen,
> Are mighty gossips in our monarchy. (76–83)

We may recall More's comment that it is highly unlikely that the "o'erworn
widow" (Queen Elizabeth) and her rival, Mistress Shore, should be on such
terms as to be "gossips." Introducing the idea this early, though, makes Richard
seem that much more clever to set up the idea of conspiracy between the two
women, not to mention the impression that the king is completely controlled
by them, early in the prosecution of his plan. Gloucester then exercises his
considerable wit on the doughty Brackenbury, who states that he has "naught
to do" with such affairs (97):

> Naught to do with Mistress Shore? I tell thee, fellow,
> He that doth naught with her (excepting one)
> Were best to do it secretly alone. (98–100)

This joke may seem oddly inappropriate in the mouth of the man who would later come over all righteous and condemn the woman of "naught" to public penance. What it illustrates, though, is the marvellous two-facedness of Shakespeare's Richard, his ability to alter his personality instantly to fit his circumstances and/or audience.

During the III.iv Tower scene Shore and the Queen become targets of something more dangerous than pleasantry:

> Look how I am bewitched; behold my arm
> Is like a blasted sapling, wither'd up;
> And this is Edward's wife, that monstrous witch,
> Consorted with that harlot, strumpet Shore,
> That by their witchcraft thus have marked me. (68-72)

This adaptability of Richard's, however, makes it difficult to make any judgment about the playwright's attitude toward Mistress Shore. After all, Gloucester is the only person to discuss her in any detail, and he is hardly a reliable witness. Given her virtual non-appearance in the play, then, and her sole dependence for representation on its chief villain, it appears that, for Shakespeare at least, Mistress Shore commanded little interest either as a subject of pathos or a moral exemplum.[1]

The True Tragedie of Richard the Third

Certainly there is no doubt about the moral attitude *of The True Tragedy of Richard the Third* (1594) regarding Mistress Shore: the full title promises, among other delights, "a Lamentable Ende of Shores Wife, an Example for All Wicked Women." The word "wicked" does not carry the same ambiguity as, say, the word "lewd."[2] We are meant to see Shore's wife as wicked, despite her appeal.

Of course, the primary villain of the piece is undoubtedly Richard; the title also promises "the Smothering of the Two Yoong Princes in the Tower," and wraps up with "the Conjunction and Joyning of the Two Noble Houses, Lancaster and Yorke." Like his contemporary William Shakespeare, the anonymous author of the "True Tragedie" toed the Tudor party line, following without question the precedent set by More regarding Richard's unquestionable guilt in the disappearance of his nephews.

The play opens with the dying King Edward attempting to reconcile the two factions in his court: the older nobility, represented by Hastings, and the upstart Woodvilles, represented by "Lord Marcus" (the Marquis of Dorset). Also taking part in the death-watch is Mistress Shore, who takes a rather cold-bloodedly practical view of her situation. Worried about her future should the king die, she reassures herself with thought of the "friends" she has brought to preferment and of her favor with the king:

> For what was it his grace would deny Shore's wife?
> Of any thing, yea, were it half his revenues,
> I know his grace would not see me want.

Nevertheless, she resolves to be more prudent in the future:

> But if the king scape, as I hope he will,
> Then will I feather my neast,
> That blow the stormie winter never so cold,
> I will be thoroughly provided for one.

Alas, Shore's wife never gets the opportunity to feather her nest, for the king indeed dies and Shore more or less disappears until invoked by Richard in his accusation of Hastings:

> … thou and that accursed sorceresse the mother Queene hath bewitched me, with assistance of that famous strumpet of my brothers, Shores wife: my withered arm is a sufficient testimony, deny it if thou canst: laie not Shore's wife with thee last night?

Hastings indignantly refutes that charge:

> That she was in my home my Lord I cannot deny, but not for any such matter.

This denial goes against the popular assumption that Hastings took Shore as his mistress after Edward's death. Probably the author of the *True Tragedie* wanted to illustrate unequivocally the disinterestedness of the noble Hastings: Shore might be under his "protection," but not in his bed.

Having disposed of Hastings, Richard then gives particularly detailed instructions regarding Shore's wife:

And now that Shores wifes goods be confiscate, goe from me to the Bishop of London, and see that she receive her open penance, let her be turned out of prison, but so bare as a wretch that worthily hath deserved that plague: and let there be straight proclamation made by my Lord the Mayor, that none shall releeve her nor pittie her, and privie spies set in everie corner of the Citie, that they may take notice of them that releeves her: for as her beginning was most famous above all, so I will have her end most infamous above all.

No particular reason is given for Richard's vindictiveness; supposedly, to a Tudor audience it is enough that he is Richard. The "privie spies" are a nice extra touch of malevolence.

Deprived of relief and "pittie," Shore's wife laments her condition:

Ay why was I made faire that a King should favour me? But my friends should have prefered discipline before affection: for they know of my folly, yea my owne husband knew of my breach of disloyaltie, and yet suffered me, by reason he knew it were bootlesse to kicke against the pricke.

This speech invokes the by now standard characteristics of Shore's downfall— her beauty, her rebelliousness, and her "friends." There is a new twist, however, in that the "friends" seem guilty, not of marrying her off too early to a man she did not love, but of too much indulgence. Her beauty drew the attention of the king, but it was apparently others' responsibility to see that Shore behaved herself. Moreover, her husband appears to have been singularly apathetic, to say the least. In the social context of the period, Shore's "friends" failed to do their proper job. The message, therefore, is not just to "Wicked Women," but to those given control over them. Parents who fail to prefer discipline over affection, and husbands who throw up their hands and decide it is "bootlesse to kicke against the pricke," violate a vital principle of the social hierarchy.

Fortune is also a very important concept in this play; both Shore and Richard invoke it repeatedly. Like the ballads, the play reminds its audience of the of the fleeting nature of prosperity in Shore's comparison of her privileged life with her destitution:

… all my friends forsake me. In prosperitie I had many, but in adversitie none. A gods have I this for my good I have done, for when I was in my cheefest pomp, I thought that day wel spent wherein I might pleasure my friend by sutes to the King, for if I had spoken he would not have said nay. For tho he was King, yet Shores wife swayed the swoord. I where need was, there was I bountifull, and mindfull I was still upon the poore to releeve them.

This passage is noteworthy for several reasons. Buried in the lament there is the strong statement, "For tho he was King, yet Shores wife swayed the swoord." Leaving aside the obvious bawdy implication (as in "kicke against the pricke"), the notion of Shore's wife wielding the sword is reminiscent of Churchyard,[3] and of More's "weighty sutes." However, it is carefully tempered fore and aft with qualifications. She gave mere "pleasure" to friends through her suits, and she ends invoking her bounty to the poor. These qualifications work to trivialize her power in the first case, and render it unexceptionable in the second. The "swoord" borne by Mistress Shore, the play assures us, was a typically "feminine" one.

   The True Tragedie of Richard the Third is not a terribly good play. Given its date, it may possibly be a rip-off of Shakespeare's. While Shakespeare only mentions Shore in passing, however, The *True Tragedie* represents her in the flesh, avowedly as "an example for All Wicked Women." Like the Shore of the ballads, however, she comes off as less intentionally wicked than constitutionally wayward. An object of pity at the hands of rotten King Richard, her power, and any threat she might pose as a former king's favorite are marginalized. Like Churchyard's Shore, she almost seems destined to sin because of her femaleness, and like Chute's she is doomed by her own beauty. The one significant contribution of this play to the growing lore of Shore's wife is the assignment of agency to her "friends" and husband for not performing their god-ordained duty of keeping her in line. Her case is indeed lamentable, but not terribly interesting. In or around 1599, however, Thomas Heywood's *First and Second Parts of King Edward the Fourth* offer an at once more complex and more active Mistress Shore.

Thomas Heywood, *King Edward IV*, Parts I and II

The adulterous wife appears to have been a subject of interest for Thomas Heywood. In addition to including Jane Shore in *King Edward IV*, Parts I and II (1599), he takes up the subject in two other plays, *A Woman Killed with Kindness* (1603) and *The English Traveller* (1631). In all these plays there can be no doubt of the inevitable condemnation of the adulteress; Heywood seems to have been particularly concerned with the sanctity of marriage, especially given his later Puritan leanings (Morton 33, 36). In this earliest of the three, however, Heywood acknowledges the extenuating circumstances of Jane Shore's defection, and with her good deeds and non-stop repentance endeavors to reflect the ambiguity of the harlot/heroine figure. In addition, he, like More, subtly criticizes Edward IV even as he acknowledges his appeal (Baines 13).

The plays also, like his own *If You Know Not Me You Know Nobody*, and "city" comedies like Dekker's *The Shoemaker's Holiday*, make London itself a character and celebrate citizen-morality somewhat at the expense of aristocratic dignity. Both Heywood and Dekker reflect the ambivalence of relations between the merchant and the aristocrat, an ambivalence that extends both ways, and is further complicated by the emergence and integration into the mix of the venture capitalist.[4]

Heywood's play reduces the first decade of Edward's reign to the conflict over his marriage with Elizabeth Woodville. The Duchess of York expresses grave concern about the political ramifications of the act which her son dismisses lightly. To her prophetic verse protestation that "that is done by you/ Which yet the child that is unborn shall rue" Edward defends his marriage in airy prose:

> Tush mother you are deceived, all true subiects shall have cause to thanke God, to have their king borne of a true Englishwoman, I tell you it was never well since wee matched with strangers, so our children have beene still like Chicken of the half kind, but where the cock and the hen be both of one breede, there is like to be birds of the game. (5)

Only when a Messenger enters, bringing news of the Falconbridge rebellion,[5] does Edward speak seriously and in verse. The juxtaposition of the marriage and the rebellion, certainly, suggests a connection between them. Certainly Edward's marriage, and the subsequent aggrandizement of the Woodville/Grey faction, was responsible in part for the defection of Warwick and the Duke of Clarence and the temporary readeption of Henry VI in 1470. Heywood, however, telescopes the action; clearly he is not interested in the King-maker, still less in brother Clarence. Falconbridge's attempt on London allows Heywood quickly to introduce the city of London, and its loyal and courageous citizens. Nevertheless, the unrest following so hard upon the marriage inevitably calls the marriage's advisability into question (Baines 13).

Heywood's positive attitude toward the citizens is evident, in the juxtaposition of two subsequent scenes. The vulgar conversation of Spicing, Chub, and co., all members of Falconbridge's force, and the noble discourse of the Lord Mayor and Master Shore reflects Heywood's understanding of the citizens' significant role in confirming Edward's rule. Crosbie and Matthew Shore represent, in fact, "model" citizens.

> Heywood shaped and affirmed the values and aspirations of the London
> citizens and delineated for them their place in a changing social and economic
> structure. (Baines 10)

This model quality, particularly of Matthew Shore, becomes more and more
evident as the text unfolds.

In no other account so far has the citizenry of London come in for such
attention. With his citizen-oriented perspective, Heywood becomes the first
interpreter of the Jane Shore story to represent her substantially as a "woman
of the people." It is important to remember that a vast majority of the English
people did not dictate the "world historical events" of the 15th century, although
they often suffered from them. The London merchantocracy from which Jane
Shore originated, however, was a key player behind the scenes of aristocratic
warfare, and had a potentially substantial impact on their outcome. It was the
Common Council of London that determined that no resistance should be
made to Edward's re-taking of the city in 1471 (Ross, *Edward* 166), and it was
the citizens who repelled Falconbridge's "substantial force" shortly thereafter
(174). Theirs was not necessarily a disinterested loyalty. The wealthy merchants
had advanced substantial loans to the crown in the 1460s, a common practice
between a commonality with ready cash and a monarch in need but reluctant
to risk the public-relations fallout usually provoked by the imposition of taxes.
The briefly readepted Henry VI was poor in both health and pocket. The King-
maker, Warwick, was unlikely to make good on debts contracted by his enemy.
Supporting Edward, therefore, was the most likely way to recover their money
(Ross, *Edward* 166). In addition, whatever his shortcomings as a king might have
been, the city esteemed Edward because "he was traditionally associated with
the middle class and with its achievement of a place in English history" (Baines
10). His liaison with Jane Shore in *Edward IV* extends that association.

Heywood also introduces a cozy domesticity into the pre-Edward
relationship between Shore and her husband. She addresses him with the
diminutive "Mat" (25) and the endearment "Sweetheart" (24) and expresses
wifely concern for his safety when he ventures out at the head of a troop of
citizens to confront Falconbridge. She also gives a rather ironic guarantee of
her chastity. Falconbridge has earlier taunted Master Shore, promising to bed
"Shore's wife, the flow'r of London" (16), and the anxious husband explains
his zeal is in part due to his fear of losing her. She objects,

> Of me sweetheart? why how should I be lost?
> Were I by thousand stormes of fortune tost,

And should endure the poorest wretched life,
Yet Jane will be thy honest, loyall wife,
The greatest Prince the Sunne did ever see
Shall never make me prove untrue to thee. (24)

The fighting over, a grateful King Edward knights the Mayor and other citizens, but Master Shore refuses the honor. Heywood again injects a note of irony with Edward's response:

Well, be it as thou wilt, some other way
We will devise to quittance thy deserts. (33)

The play then temporarily leaves the city and follows Edward on light-hearted frolic in the country. The popular tradition has Edward fond of disguise and incognito appearances among his people; the popular ballad "King Edward IV and the Tanner of Tamworth"[6] is an example of this predilection and is the basis of this particular plot line in Part I of *King Edward IV*. The fondness for disguise and role-playing established here reappears later in the King's courtship of Mistress Shore.

This courtship follows very much along the lines of Michael Drayton's two poems, with two important exceptions. She is, like Drayton's Shore, Edward's match in verbal sophistication. Much of the flirtation language is similar, leading to the presumption that either Heywood or Drayton was familiar with the other's text, or that there is a no-longer-extant "Q" text to which they both referred. The "jewel" language is once more prominent: The king, heavily cloaked and posing as a potential customer, asks for "Your fairest jewel, be it not too dear" (64). Shore replies, also euphemistically, "I see you come to cheape and not to buy" (65). A series of double-entendres follows, until Edward reveals who he is and Master Shore enters shortly thereafter.

Other similarities between the two works abound: Drayton's Edward speaks of Master Shore as "having all, yet knowes not what is had" (21). When, in Heywood's play, Jane declares that her husband, though in possession of "what you rate so high ... yet is still the poorer by the match" Edward answers, "That easily proves he doth not know the worth" (65). Drayton's Edward says her beauty "Is like an un-cut Diamond in lead (28); Heywood's calls her "Bright twinkling spark of precious diamond." Drayton's expansively vows, " So much is Beautie pleasing unto all,/ That Prince and Pesant equally doth call;/ Nor never yet did any Man despise it,/ Except too deare, and that he could not prize it" (119–22): Heywood's Edward qualifies his request for her "fairest jewel" with "be it not too dear."

The "courtly" nature of Heywood's exchange has a rather different effect than in Drayton, however. In Drayton's poem, as noted above, the linguistically sophisticated nature of the exchange, coupled with the complaints about city husbands, serves to distance Jane Shore from her merchant origins. She appears too good for the lumpish, jealous man who "possesses" her. In Heywood's play, however, Jane's elegance is of a piece with the natural refinement of the citizens as a group. Drayton disparages the city; Heywood celebrates it.

The second exception involves the manner of Jane's ultimate surrender to Edward. Drayton's Shore is an already discontented wife, clearly above her husband's paltry jealousies; by the end of her "Epistle" she declares herself "conquered" by her royal besieger. Heywood's Edward has to work quite a bit harder. There are two scenes of courtship, between which Mistress Shore seeks the not-very-helpful advice of Mistress Blague. She has clearly been shaken by the first encounter: although she has denied the king in his first attempt, she has also denied to her husband that the mysterious stranger importuning her is the king. She closes the scene with the assurance, "No king thats under heaven Ile love like thee," but "Mat" Shore's misgivings are heavily prophetic, and invoke the now-familiar distrust of beauty:

> Keep we our treasure secret, yet so fond,
> As set so rich a beautie as this is
> In the wide view of every gazers eye.
> Oh traitor beautie, Oh deceitfull good!
> That both conspire against thyself and love,
> No sooner got, but wisht againe of others!
> In thine owne self injurious to thy self!
> Oh rich poor portion! thou good evill thing!
> How many joyful woes still both thou bring! (68)

As in Chute, there is something inherently fatal in "beautie." It is inevitably treacherous, regardless of its possessor.

The sense of almost hypnotic inevitability established by Master Shore's speech is heightened in the scene with Mistress Blague. Mistress Shore has summoned her friend in distress, having received letters from the king which intimate that he will not take "no" for an answer. Mistress Blague seems initially on the side of chastity, invoking all the ill effects of surrender: loss of her good name, her husband's disgrace, and her piteous state if/when the king loses interest in her. At the conclusion of the speech, however, she retreats into the non-committal rhyming couplet, "Yet I will not be she shall counsel ye,/ Good Mistress Shore do what ye will for me" (73). From here she launches into a series of devil's advocate speeches, suggesting various attractions of the proposition: the sin would be less given the greatness of the man who engendered it; the potential advancement of herself and her family; her power to do good; the superior protection of a king's favor; and finally, the attractions of court life. And each speech is punctuated by the monotonous, sing-song disclaimer:

> Yet I will not be she shall counsel ye,
> Good Mistress Shore do what ye will for me. (74–5)

The scene ends with the king's return and Mistress Blague retires, uttering a final "counsel:"

> Now Mistress Shore bethink ye what to do,
> Such suitors come not every day to woo. (75)

The second encounter between the King and Mistress Shore begins very much like the first; the two of them bandy double-entendres, she keeping his declarations at bay with metaphor and philosophical rhetoric. But the king abruptly puts a stop to her evasions:

> But, leaving this our enigmaticke talke,
> Thou must sweete Jane, repaire unto the court,
> His tongue intreates, controules the greatest peer:
> His hand plights love, a royall scepter holdes;
> And in his heart hee hath confirmd thy good,
> Which may not, must not, shal not be withstood. (76)

The thinly-veiled invocation of prerogative is not lost on Jane, who replies,

> If you enforce me, I have nought to say
> But wish I had not livde to see this day.

Edward advises that he will send for her that evening, and promises her "cause to joy" and advancement. He takes his leave with a pledge of his benign intentions:

> In sign whereof receive this true-love kisse,
> Nothing ill meant, there can be no amisse.

Left alone, Jane resigns herself to her new condition:

> Well I will in, and ere the time beginne,
> Learne how to be repentant for my sinne. (76)

The psychology of Mistress Shore's surrender is complicated, although a bit less so than that of Heywood's Mistress Frankford in *A Woman Killed*.[7] The strong insinuation of constraint at the end of the encounter, like Master Shore's discourse on beauty, seems to mitigate Jane's "sinne." Nevertheless, she accepts it as such, and dutifully answers the king's summons when it comes. In the next scene Master Shore is told, simply, by the boy,

> Maister, my Mistresse by a Nobleman
> Is sent for to the king in a close Coach,
> Shee's gone with him, these are the newes I bring. (78)

The suddenness of Mistress Shore's capitulation, like Mistress Frankford's, is somewhat dissatisfying psychologically, but makes sense artistically. From the beginning, as the title promises, it is inevitable that Mistress Shore will become the King's concubine; she has to in order for the plot to go on. Everyone in the audience knows the story; like Anne Frankford's, Jane Shore's infidelity is predetermined.[8]

In an echo of the first scene of the play, Master Shore, Francis Emersly and the Lord Mayor speculate on the political ramifications of Edward's love life. Just as his marriage to Elizabeth Woodville put an end to an advantageous foreign alliance, Edward's diversions with tanners and city wives are distracting him from more important doings.

> I wonder in this serious busie time
> Of this great gathered Benevolence
> For his regaining of his right in France,
> The day and nightly turmoile of his lordes,
> Yea of the whole estate in generall,
> He can be spared from these great affaires
> And wander here disguised in this sort. (78)

Emersly's words remind us that Edward raised a substantial sum—this time via taxation ("this great gathered benevolence")—for the express purpose of invading France. These taxes had been reluctantly granted by Parliament, which had twice before voted taxes for such a purpose without results. On both previous occasions Edward had come to terms with the enemy and the moneys had somehow ended up covering miscellaneous royal expenditures (Ross, *Edward* 215). Any apparent lack of seriousness on the part of Edward in this third attempt could be politically damaging. Heywood's is the first text to foreground explicitly the fiscal aspect of Edward's political inadequacies, which Heywood clearly links to his pleasure-seeking personality. Although, indeed, there were many serious diplomatic setbacks which accounted for Edward's delay in the current invasion (Ross, *Edward* 223–6), Heywood reduces them to his obsession with Jane Shore. The conflict between the "king's two bodies"—the personal and political—is specifically sexual in this play, but it is specifically Edward's and not Jane's sexuality which is at issue. Both Matthew and Jane Shore here seem passive objects of the king's will.

Matthew's passivity in particular is manifest in the scene near the close of the first part of *Edward IV*. In it Mistress Shore, "Lady-like attired," encounters her husband as he is about to embark on a voyage abroad. To his declaration that she is now "nor widdow, maide or wife" she acknowledges that she "yeelded up the forte/ Wherein lay all the riches of thy joy." She professes herself ready, however, to "yeeld it backe againe" and join him in exile (84). But Master Shore will have none of it:

> Thou go with me, Jane, Oh God forbid
> That I should be a traitor to my king!
> Shall I become a felon to his pleasures,
> And fly away as guiltie of the theft?
> No my dear Jane, I say it may not be.
> Oh, what have subjects that is not their kings,
> Ile not examine his prerogative. (84–5)

She still tries to persuade him to stay, promising him wealth through her influence with the King: "What ist with Edward that I cannot doe?" She has already in the scene demonstrated her power in her disposal of a number of suits. She has, in short order, delivered a pardon to one man, promised the restitution of lands to another two (defraying one's expenses by arranging for him to board with the king's servants), and stingingly rebuked Rufford's application for a patent to transport corn and lead abroad:

> I had your bill; but I have torne your bill;
> And twere no shame, I think, to teare your eares,
> That care not how you wound the commonwealth.
> The poor must starve for foode, to fill your purse,

> And the enemy bandy bullets of our leade!
> No, maister Rufford, Ile not speake for you,
> Except it be to have you punished! (83)

These suits may or may not be "weighty," to use Thomas More's term, but the discrimination Heywood attributes to Shore, and her sensitivity to suitors' immediate needs, suggests integrity and precision of thought, and render her a worthy conduit for the king's favors. She stubbornly refuses reward, moreover, preferring to do good for its own sake; she does not even see it as a mitigation of her adultery:

> No, without gifts, God grant I may do good.
> For all my good cannot redeeme my ill;
> Yet to do good I will endevour still. (82)

Master Shore, however, despises to rise by his shame. He embarks for the Continent with a final parting shot:

> Adieu, O world, he shall deceived be,
> That puts his trust in women or in thee. (85)

The scene perfectly articulates the double-bind endured by Jane Shore, the juxtaposition of harlot and heroine in one figure. The implicit constraint of her situation is further established by Master Shore's bitter declaration that the king's pleasure is paramount; that anything a subject possesses—including a wife—is itself subject to seizure by the Crown. Yet though Jane turns her situation to account by using her position actively to do good, no amount of good can redeem her "ill": finally, she is subject to the blanket condemnation that women are simply not to be trusted. More explicitly than any other representation of Jane Shore, Heywood's play highlights the irreconcilable contradiction of her position.

Futhermore, Heywood heightens this contradiction with Shore's problematic status as a political player. While she on one hand rewards worthy suitors and rejects unworthy ones, she is only recognized by others as a distraction from the "serious busie time," not as a part of it. Heywood intensifies this tension between the personal and the political in the second part of *Edward IV*, placing Shore at the edge of events, but unconscious of her influence, if any, on them. Some time has passed since the end of the first part. Edward prosecutes his adventure in France despite the treachery of the Duke of Burgundy, and the affair ends in the Treaty of Picquigny, which

Heywood represents as a "victory" for England.[9] When we finally return to the domestic front, Master Shore, newly returned from his travels and bearing the alias Flood, is, along with his travelling companions, sentenced to die as a pirate. Jane Shore acquires a pardon for the company at the request of Lord Brackenbury, whose cousin is the captain. Brackenbury subsequently takes on "Flood" as a servant, which keeps him close to the center of his wife's affairs without her knowledge for the rest of the play.

This portion of this rendition of the Jane Shore story is remarkable chiefly for a confrontation scene between Shore and Queen Elizabeth. Perhaps wanting to make Richard's "conspiracy theory" more plausible, Heywood imagines a scene in which Elizabeth Woodville begins by threatening and upbraiding her rival, but is so disarmed by the latter's humility and penitence that she ends embracing Shore and showering her with kisses. The scene concludes with the two women promising mutual aid and support.[10]

The bulk of the rest of the play involves Gloucester's usurpation of the throne after the death of his brother. The Shore material follows fairly familiar lines with a couple of exceptions. The first is that Flood, Master Shore in disguise, is, because of his position as Brackenbury's servant, on the spot at the Tower of London when Tyrrell and the murderers discharge Brackenbury from his duty in order to assassinate the princes. There is a fight, and Flood is wounded. He next appears in the home of Mistress Blague, to which Jane also has repaired, fleeing from the Protector. Suspension of disbelief is stretched to the limit here when Jane tends Flood's wounds and fails to recognize him as her husband. This convenient amnesia assures that Flood will once again be on the spot when Brackenbury arrives with the news of Jane's imminent arrest and penance. The edict further instructs that she be turned out of any lodging, and that anyone who tries to succor her will be hanged as a traitor. Mistress Blague immediately turns against her erstwhile friend, and takes possession of the jewels and goods Jane has left in her safekeeping.

Unlike the Jane Shores of ballad and poetry, Heywood's does not repine at length over the vicissitudes of fortune. Instead, she interprets her condition as a just punishment for having disgraced *London*:

> Farewell to thee, where first I was enticde
> That scadalizde thy dignity with shame;
> But now thou hast returnd me treble blame;
> London! thy flints have punisht for their pride,
> And thou hast drunke their blood for thy revenge.
> What now avails to think what I have beene?
> Then welcome nakedness and poverty! (165–66)

Here again the pride of the city and the citizen show through in Heywood's work in a way that the story has never reflected before. More than a simplistic moral tale, the play reflects a consciousness of the ethical superiority of the honest, hard-working citizen, and the woe inevitable to anyone who strays from that ideal. The only citizen villains in the play, Mistress Blague and Rufford, explicitly violate the city ethos by attempting to gain wealth through trickery, not honest labor.[11] Mistress Blague betrays and cheats her friend, but she too is paid in kind, for she becomes a beggar alongside Mistress Shore. Rufford acquires his patents by forgery, and curries favor with King Richard by betraying to him those who would, against the edict, give Shore relief. He in turn is exposed by Master Shore and led off to his death.

When Shore/Flood comes to the aid of his estranged wife, he too is arrested and taken before Richard. Before the king he relinquishes his alias and claims the right to succor Jane on the basis of their relationship. Richard at first appears willing to grant this, but only conditionally:

> Except thou thake her home againe to thee,
> Thou art a stranger, and it shall not be,
> For if thou do, expect what doth belong.
> To this, however, Master Shore is unwilling to agree:
> I never can forget so great a wrong.

Shore/Flood cites his "compassion" as an alternatively valid motivation, but Richard is firm:

> Then never feede her whom thou canst not love. (179)

Master Shore's integrity here seems arbitrary, but is very much of a piece with Heywood's morality. The trouble is, what *is* that morality? Again, the example *of A Woman Killed* is useful here. Master Frankford's utter rejection of his wife is non-negotiable; yet he does not condemn her to death. Although in both cases the husbands' rejection results in the *de facto* death of their wives, it is not by their direct action. This may be an explicit vindication of the husbands,[12] or an implicit critique of them.[13]

The play ends with both husband and wife dying, side by side, once again "married" in death:

> Oh, dying marriage! oh, sweet married death
> Thou grave, which only shouldst part faithful friends,
> Bringst us togither, and dost joine our hands.

Oh, living death! even in this dying life,
Yet, ere I go, once, Matthew, kiss thy wife.

He kisseth her, and she dies. (183)

The husband outlives the wife only long enough to once again denounce the world and the power of kings:

Oh, unconstant world,
Here lies a true anatomie of thee,
A king had all my joy, that her enjoyed,
And by a king again she was destroyed.
All ages of my kingly woes shall tell.
Once more, inconstant world farewell, farewell. *He dyes.* (183)

Each of these three plays treats Jane Shore as a peripheral character, but they all acknowledge her significance as an integral part of the story of the last Plantagenets. A trend emerges, however, which reveals the different authors' priorities in representing the events of the 1480s, and the place they give the harlot/heroine in those events. For Shakespeare, Richard is clearly the focus, and Mistress Shore provides a vehicle for illustrating the cleverness and opportunistic quality of his villainy. The *True Tragedie*'s Shore exemplifies the fickleness of fortune, but also suggests a certain justice in the fall of a citizen's wife who intended—though too late—to feather her "neast" through the influence of the king. Both of these women's political activity, such as it is, derives from their sexual relationship with the king, but that relationship itself is elided for the most part. There is little sense of Shore herself as a sexual agent; her status as an adulteress is a given, but not a focus. Her position is more or less straightforward; it evokes little ambiguity.

Heywood's Shore is entirely different. The two seduction scenes with Edward are erotic and explicitly sexual. Her adultery is further foregrounded by the scene of confrontation with Queen Elizabeth, and the scenes with her husband: when she initially lies to him about the king's identity, when she offers to join him in exile, and in his almost non-stop commentary after his return from abroad as Flood. Heywood never lets us, or Shore herself, forget that she is a adulteress. If that aspect of her is enhanced, however, so is her charity.[14] Heywood actually shows us examples of Shore's benevolence, some of which have clearly political implications (the refusal of the patent to Rufford, and the pardon for the "pirates" who unknowingly violated Edward's treaty with France). Master Shore himself articulates the ambiguity of her position when he claims his right as her husband to relieve her in want, but refuses to take her to him as his wife again.

For Shakespeare and the author of the *True Tragedie*, it is the larger-than-life Richard who fascinates by virtue of his sheer villainy. Heywood at once presents a more complex and less satisfying story, one more life-like than the others, one suspects. No one in Heywood's play—except perhaps Master Shore—is free from fault: Edward plays when he ought to work; Queen Elizabeth is proud; Mistress Blague turns out to be a fair-weather friend. And though Jane Shore declares that "to doe good I will endeavor still," she knows that "all my good cannot redeeme my ill" (82). Heywood doesn't want our pity to overcome our understanding. However, Jane is not merely a "lesson" as she seems to be in the ballads, or if she is, it is directed at someone other than rebellious women. It is directed at a nobility which should know its place and its responsibilities, and not take either lightly; it is directed at a citizenry whose importance the nobility ought to recognize, and whose morality it would do them well to imitate. It reflects a consciousness of turn-of-the-century-London that is increasingly seeing its king and itself as partners in the conduct of England's affairs. The first two plays look backward, more or less repeating the chronicle tradition, and seeing the story very much in the light of a conflict between two branches of the nobility, specifically the hereditary barons and the Queen's family. Heywood, however, looks forward, to the decline of aristocratic prerogative and the rise of the civil servant. It is this play, rather than Shakespeare's, which sets up the middle-class consciousness that will pervade the story in its 18th-century manifestations.

Notes

[1]   Helgerson notes that Shakespeare resists the "affective power" of the story deliberately, eliding Shore from his adaptation of the chronicle history (35). In doing so, he runs counter to the already powerful trend toward the intersection of the personal and the political, the domestic and the civic.

[2]   This is the word ascribed to Shore and to the women targeted by the "Woefull Lamentation." In the Oxford English dictionary, the definition of "lewd" as "Unlearned, unlettered, untaught" is given prior to "Rude, artless" and "common, low, vulgar, 'base'."

[3]   "I bare the sword though he did weare the crowne" (171).

[4]   See Straznicky 364.

[5]   Ross, *Edward* 173–4.

[6]   See Percy's *Reliques*, Vol. II.

[7]   "By largely avoiding the question of motivation, Heywood presents the act of adultery in its simplest form, unobscured by either mitigating or damning circumstances, so that we may focus without distraction on the events that follow—Anne's repentence and Frankford's 'kindness'" (Panek 368).

8   "Critics have generally been puzzled by the lack of motivation for Anne's fall. Here Heywood is less concerned with the seduction as such or its dramatic possibilities—as, for example, Shakespeare is in Richard III—than with its consequences" (Born-Lechleitner 90–91).

9   Which it wasn't. See Ross, *Edward* 234 ff.

10   "Shore's final forgiveness of his wife's adultery is foreshadowed in the scene between Queen Elizabeth and Jane Shore, which is one of Heywood's additions to the historical material...By implication, Heywood conveys that more than one household is affected by the king's adultery, although he is careful to leave out the political dimension. Just like Jane herself, the Queen is of bourgeois origin and therefore also associated with middle-class morality ... Elizabeth has internalized the teachings about wifely docility and prefers to join forces with Jane" (Born-Lechleitner 87).

11   As in *The Shoemaker's Holiday,* "the play appears to be ... condemning some and condoning other commercial enterprises, and making the distinction in terms of generosity" (Straznicky 364).

12   "The Christian context of the play demands that the death of an adulterous woman be self-inflicted and not the result of a rash action on the part of her offended husband. Death is seen as the due punishment for female adultery, yet it should be the consequence of a realization of the enormity of the sin and of repentance for it. When death is imminent, the sin of adultery fully atoned for and forgiven by Heaven, it is also possible for a wronged husband, God's representative in the family, to forgive his wife" (Born-Lechleitner 81).

13   In "Punishing Adultery in *A Woman Killed With Kindness*" Jennifer Panek assembles a convincing body of contemporary literary evidence—including material by Heywood himself—that calls into question the intransigence of the husbands.

14   "Despite her sin, Jane has tried to preserve her personal integrity throughout the play. She has constantly placed moral considerations above human, arbitrary law as embodied by the two kings who prove to be her undoing...Heywood thus tries to show the proper *contemptus mundi* attitude towards arbitrary actions of fate and of kings" (Born-Lechleitner 86).

Chapter 4

Prosaic Morality: or, Jane Shore "Explained"

Jane Shore as a subject of popular culture more or less retires temporarily during the 17th century. The extreme political and social upheaval of English society no doubt had something to do with this. As a figure of sexual instability, Shore was ironically too tame for the Jacobean and Caroline stage, which went in for increasingly bizarre examples of sexual irregularity. These reflected a growing sense of a disordered and potentially chaotic social and theological turmoil and disillusion (Born-Lechleitner 35–43).

Politically, the "pillow talk" aspect of the Shore/Edward liaison was either too topical for representation, or not topical enough, depending on one's perspective. James' extra-marital forays were more likely with persons of his own gender. His relationship with the Duke of Buckingham generated bitterness similar to the hereditary nobility's resentment of Elizabeth Woodville: Buckingham, like Elizabeth, used his personal influence to enrich and ennoble his own relatives. He also held considerable sway over Charles I until his assassination in 1629, after which Charles' Queen, Henrietta Maria, became a focus of suspicion on account of her French and Catholic origins, and Charles' devotion to her raised complaints of his "uxoriousness," and fear of her influence. Re-presentations of a king's mistress, under these circumstances, would have been a tricky business.

By the time the Civil Wars erupted in 1642, and throughout the wranglings of the Interregnum, poetry and broadsides were overshadowed by commentaries and polemics on the fluctuating authority structure and the proliferation of religious sects and political parties. The theaters were closed, and the courtier poets of the Caroline years turned their attention to attempts at epic allegories for the "troubles." The restoration of the Stuart Monarchy in 1660 did very little to solve the problems of the previous reign. All the English appear to have learned from their republican experiment is that a bad king was better than no king at all. The polarization between Court and City, between Crown and Parliament interests, was particularly evident in the newly opened theaters, which for the rest of the 17th century were the almost exclusive resort of the Court faction.

Although many of the comedies presented there represented aristocrats taking revenge on Parliamentarian citizens by cuckolding them, Court mistresses (as opposed to casual whores) seem more often to have been drawn from the aristocracy or from the ranks of the newly-established actresses, than from the merchantocracy. It is in court circles, however, that Jane Shore first reappears.

The competition between court mistresses appears to have been a matter of some amusement to onlookers. One poem circulated in the 1682 comments upon these cat-fights with particular reference to Shore: It was called "A Dialogue between the D[uchess] of C[leveland] and the D[uchess] of P[ortsmouth] at their meeting in Paris, with the Ghost of Jane Shore." In rhyming triplets, Shore's ghost declares to the rival Duchesses that she "once was such as you;/ I was a whore a Royal Mistress too./ I was a woman of Egregious fame/ And like you two I gloried in my shame." She then warns them that they, like she, will be "Tormented in the flames of hell below,/ No ease from Torment pain and endless woe,/ For pleasure past my scorchéd soul doth know." Ultimately, however, the tone of the poem overall, despite Portsmouth's claims to power and influence, is dismissive. A royal mistress, be she a Duchess or a citizen's wife, is merely a "whore," and not worth getting too excited about. The lampoon does not appear to have been exceptional; there is a similar "dialogue" between Portsmouth and Nell Gwynn, in which the former taunts the latter on account of her low birth and the latter degrades the former's pernicious influence as a Frenchwoman.

An earlier poem, Samuel Butler's "New Ballad" (1671) has a similarly light touch. It is a catalogue of women from antiquity, the Bible, and popular literature, all of dubious reputations. Short verses summarizing their impact on their male victims are punctuated with the more or less nonsense refrain:

> Jane Shore she was for England, Queen Fredrick was for
> France;
> Sing Honi soit qui mal y pense.

At the end, King Edward IV is deemed as sorry a hero as any in history:

> Warlike Penthesilea was an Amazonian Whore
> To Hector and young Troilus, both which did her adore;
> But Brave King Edward, who before had gain'd nine Victories
> Was like a Bond-slave fetter'd within Jane Shore's All
> conquering Thighs.

Although these poems do not foreground serious political consequences of a king's amorous adventures, underlying both are deeply-embedded cultural prejudices regarding the intersection between sex and politics: the working-class Gwynn, for example, suggests she is a less dangerous liaison than the high-born Portsmouth because she is at least English. And Butler's poem plays heavily on the stereotypical weakness of even the bravest, strongest of men caught between a woman's thighs.

But if representation of Jane Shore flagged somewhat in the 17th century, it positively burgeoned, along with other literary work, in the 18th, and her representation reflects some distinct artistic and social developments. The first is a rise in secular print culture, generated for a reading public that had dramatically increased. With all these "new" readers, different kinds of texts began to emerge. The elite, Augustan reader, of course, stuck to the classical humanist model of literature. He (and he was more or less always "he") saw writing as a primarily artistic, rhetorical skill, as practiced by the great authors of ancient Greece and Rome. But the more humble sort of reader, the apprentice with (perhaps) a grammar-school education, or the female servant who learned her letters at a dame-school, had different needs, and the booksellers moved quickly to fill them. The desire for "novel," as in "new" narratives manifested itself in compact, readable prose forms. A new generation of chap-books, these could be morally instructive, informative, or simply sensational (Hunter 86–7). Writers of both the "ancient" and "modern" persuasion are represented in the Jane Shore corpus, but the split is by no means an absolute one. Although I will treat Nicholas Rowe's *The Tragedy of Jane Shore* and the "histories" that follow as "ancient" and "modern," respectively, neither the play nor the narratives fit those categories neatly. These were texts written for the market, not for literary debate.

On an artistic level, "sensibility" was a characteristic valued especially by the Augustans. Augustan writers like Swift and Pope certainly reveled in satire, but others, like Steele and Addison, also understood the appeal of pathos to early 18th-century theater audiences. The pathetic potential of Jane Shore attracted the playwright Nicholas Rowe and made his play, *The Tragedy of Jane Shore*, an instant success in 1714. Rowe's play proclaims itself as neo-classical, with its set speeches, its commitment to the "unities," and its nostalgia for pastoral retreat. Nevertheless, for all its Shakespearian referentiality and rejection of urban values, it still reflects the now-irreversible triumph of what has been called middle-class morality over hereditary *noblesse oblige*.

In the 16th century, poems, plays, and ballads had dutifully acknowledged the moral deficiency of their heroine, but had not seen it as problematic in terms of representing her. In the 18ᵗʰ century, however, her ambivalent moral status does pose a problem for the playwright:

> Here is then a strange Contrast of Images, and Variety of Incidents, that make this Character, tho' vitious, yet pleasing; and so pleasing, as to force us to a Condolance of her Misery, almost as much as if her Character were free from Faults, and entirely Virtuous. (Aikins 259)

Extremes are quite apparent in Rowe's *Jane Shore*. Where Drayton referred to the relationship between Edward and Mistress Shore as merely "unlawful," and Heywood hints at coercion as a mitigating circumstance, the judgment of this critic pronounces the character "vitious;" at the same time she is irresistibly compelling. And while More, though a saint-in-waiting, seemed unwilling to judge a king's mistress harshly, her harlot/heroine dualism stands out in greater relief in the literary and social climate of the Augustan period.

What is that climate and how does the play reflect it? A cultivation of refinement, or "politeness," was certainly part of it. The rather coarse exchange about Mistress Shore between Gloucester and Clarence at the beginning of Shakespeare's *Richard III* would have been out of place in 1714. And if, as Pratt reminds us, "More granted a king the right to have a mistress" (1294), the cozily domestic reigns of William and Mary, and Anne, had established a less indulgent climate.

This is also the age of Enlightenment, at the beginning of which, at least, some of the frantic activity of the past hundred years gave way for a while to minute examination of the mind and the world in which it lived. While Heywood's characters are primarily active and not much given to reflection, Rowe's are continually examining and describing the state of their feelings. Very little actually *happens* in Rowe's play as opposed to the almost frenetic activity in *Edward IV*, but a great deal is felt, and felt deeply.

There is no absence of ambivalence or contradiction, however. While *Edward IV* had aspects of domestic tragedy within a larger political framework, *The Tragedy of Jane Shore* seems primarily domestic, but at the same time Shore's explicitly political activity is specifically invoked as a cause of her downfall at the hands of Richard III. This serves to complicate rather than simplify the representation of the harlot/heroine. While Rowe's Jane Shore agonizes continually about her sinful past, making it impossible for us to forget it, her advocacy on behalf of Edward's sons renders her a more significant political player than Heywood's, whose activity seems limited to granting or withholding patents and reversing or reducing harsh sentences.

Finally, and ultimately most striking, the ethos of the play has subtly altered to suit the times. While Heywood applauds the innate nobility of the citizenry in Edward IV, there is still no doubt as to the license afforded to the hereditary nobility. Edward's behaviour may be irresponsible and unfair, but even the upright Matthew Shore concedes that a king may do what an ordinary man may not. In Rowe's play the critique of Edward is softened by his absence from the play proper, but the language describing him is harsh, and Lord Hastings, as the primary representative of hereditary nobility, is seriously flawed.

While Rowe announced the play as "Written in Imitation of Shakespeare's Style," few critics have taken the claim seriously. Certainly the famous tower scene in which Richard accuses Hastings of treason is much as it is in Shakespeare; but the play shows obvious indebtedness to *Edward IV* and, perhaps, to other popular sources. Structurally, the play is much more in accord with the classical precepts of the Augustan stage than any of Shakespeare's plays: there are no sub-plots, and the action is compressed into a very brief span of time. The effect of these structural alterations is enormous.

First, because of Rowe's adherence to the unity of time, we come upon Jane Shore only after Edward's death. We do not witness his wooing, or her behaviour as his mistress. This has an effect of distancing Shore from her "sin," since she is already in the throes of misery and remorse when we first see her. Edward's charm is almost entirely absent from the play; at the same time, the implication of coercion in Heywood's text is heightened and more strongly expressed. In Act V, Master Shore, who, like his counterpart in Edward IV has returned home incognito after a long absence, describes his wife's desertion to their mutual friend Bellmour:

> I met her, Bellmour, when the royal spoiler
> Bore her in triumph from my widowed home!
> Within his chariot by his side she sate
> And listened to his talk with downward looks,
> Till sudden, as she chanced aside to glance,
> Her eyes encountered mine. —Oh, then, my friend!
> Oh, who can paint my grief and her amazement!
> As at the stroke of death, twice turned she pale,
> And twice a burning crimson blushed all o'er her;
> Then, with a shriek heart-wounding, loud she cried,
> While down her cheeks two gushing torrents ran
> Fast falling on her hands, which thus she wrung.
> Moved at her grief, the tyrant ravisher
> With courteous action wooed her oft to turn;

Earnest he seemed to plead, but all in vain;
Ev'n to the last she bent her signt towards me. (V.85–100)

Bellmour, agreeing, assures him,

And though the king by force possessed her person,
Her unconsenting heart dwelt still with you. (103–4)

The language used to describe King Edward, and the invocation of Shore's
"unconsenting heart," reflect a culture less even less inclined than Chute's[1]
to put up with *droigt de seigneur*. The state of Shore's heart, too, reflects an
even more complex understanding of the relationship between will and body
than in the 16th-century representations. The body may still be subject, but
neither the mind n*or* the heart is.

The behaviour of Master Shore (disguised as "Dumont") reflects the very
different understanding of authority quite early in the play. Hastings declares
his "love" for Shore passionately in Act II and, impatient with her professions
of renewed chastity, attempts to rape her. Dumont intervenes and the two
quarrel:

Lord Hastings
Avaunt! base groom;
At distance wait and know thy office better.
                         Dumont
Forgo your hold, my lord! 'tis most unmanly
This violence
                    Lord Hastings
                         Avoid the room this moment,
Or I will tread thy soul out.

                    Dumont
                         No, my lord;
The common ties of manhood call me now,
And bid me thus stand up in the defense
Of an oppressed, unhappy, helpless woman.
                    Lord Hastings
And dost thou know me? Slave!
                    Dumont
                         Yes, thou proud lord!
I know thee well, know thee with each advantage
Which wealth, or power, or noble birth can give thee.

I know thee, too, for one who stains those honors,
And blots a long illustrious line of ancestry,
By poorly daring thus to wrong a woman. (II.242–54)

A few lines later, both men draw swords and fight. Dumont wins, disarming his opponent, and then politely renders back Hastings' weapon with galling courtesy:

> Dumont
> Now, haughty sir, where is our difference now?
> Your life is in my hand, and did not honor,
> The gentleness of blood, and inborn virtue
> (Howe'er unworthy I may seem to you)
> Plead in my bosom, I should take the forfeit.
> But wear your sword again; and know, a lord
> Opposed against a man is but a man. (274–80)

This is a far cry from the passive Matthew Shore who feels that to accept his wife's offer to leave the country with him would be treason. For an Elizabethan citizen to draw a sword on a nobleman—even to possess a sword—was highly illegal. For the commoner actually to win such a contest would have been unthinkable in Heywood's England.

Shore/Dumont, in keeping with his remarks about the "tyrant ravisher," is also more forgiving than his counterpart in Heywood's play. The latter claims his right as Shore's husband to assist her in want, but steadfastly refuses to take her again as his wife. Shore/Dumont, however, hushes her self-reproaches:

> Cast every black and guilty thought behind thee,
> And let 'em never vex thy quiet more.
> My arms, my heart are open to receive thee,
> To bring thee back to thy forsaken home
> With tender joy, with fond, forgiving love,
> And all the longings of my first desires.

This "happy ending" does not, of course, come to pass. Jane Shore once again expires in her husband's arms.

In another plot deviation, Rowe's heroine plays a role in the Gloucester conspiracy. Instead of implying that Richard has made up for his own benefit the conspiracy theory linking Hastings with Shore and Queen Elizabeth, Rowe has Richard receive a letter warning him (falsely) of their plot against him.

This Richard decides to take advantage of the letter's assertion of Hastings' obsession with Shore, and offers to restore her possessions on the condition that she use her influence with Hastings to obtain his cooperation in—or at least an elimination of his resistance to—Richard's usurpation of the throne. She, of course, refuses to participate in the disenfranchisement of Edward's sons; this partisanship is the beginning of a trend in subsequent texts to imagine a close relationship between Shore and the young princes, despite the fact she has supplanted their mother in their father's affections.

Taken together, these developments of the story seem to reflect a more sophisticated—"modern," if you will—understanding of social and sexual relations. There is the further elision of distinction between the nobility and the commoners, the intensified consciousness of a mind/body split, the amplification of coercion in the account of Edward's seduction, and Shore's real and not just manufactured involvement in the succession plot. Surprisingly, however, the collective effect is actually to marginalize Shore as an active agent in her own story! Indeed, Jane Shore as Nicholas Rowe imagines her is primarily *in*active. She is a person to whom things happen; even in standing up to Richard her resistance is characterized by a refusal to act. As a heroine of tragedy, then, she is a somewhat frustrating one. If the impelling action of tragedy is the central figure's "tragic error," Rowe's text only highlights the more politically complicated double bind that confronted women in the Early Modern period. Jane Shore spends the entire play repenting a sin in which her own complicity is questionable. Moreover, any potentially redemptive activities such as are described in the 16th-century texts are unavailable to her, either because the play is limited to the portion of her career when any power she had has evaporated, or because the only active options available are ones of resistance, to Hastings' sexual advances and to Richard's political dealing.

Shore's position, in this play, is thus subject largely to the acts and commentary of others. She has been more or less kidnapped by Edward, is sexually assaulted by Hastings, persecuted by Richard, and dependent for protection and advice on Shore/Dumont. Moreover, her subject-position is compounded by the ultimate ineffectiveness of the only thing she can *do*, which is sincerely repent her past life. At the end of the play, having watched her expire in her husband's arms and seen the latter dragged off to execution for disobeying Richard's edict, Bellmour, who acts as a kind of chorus throughout, pronounces the final judgment:

> Let those who view this sad example know
> What fate attends the broken marriage vow;

> And teach their children in succeeding times,
> No common vengeance waits upon these crimes,
> When such severe repentence could not save,
> From want, from shame, and an untimely grave. (V.435–40)

The privileged position of this moral suggests that Bellmour is Rowe's representative, and/or speaks for "society." However, the logic here is strained. Judging by this "moral," one might easily presume that this is a play about adultery, but it is not, no more than is Heywood's *A Woman Killed With Kindness*. Rather, it is a more complex reflection of a cultural double-standard which depends on both condemnation and titillation.

Rowe exibits a fairly sophisticated awareness of his heroine's ambivalent position, and of Western culture's hypocrisy. He articulates it first through Jane Shore herself in her speech which closes Act I:

> Mark by what partial justice we are judged;
> Such is the fate unhappy women find,
> And such the curse entailed upon our kind,
> That man, that lawless libertine, may rove
> Free and unquestioned through the wilds of love;
> While woman, sense and nature's easy fool,
> If poor, weak woman swerve from virtue's rule,
> If, strongly charmed, she leave the thorny way,
> And in the softer paths of pleasure stray,
> Ruin ensues, reproach and endless shame,
> And one false step entirely damns her fame.
> In vain with tears the loss she may deplore,
> In vain look back to what she was before;
> She sets, like stars that fall, to rise no more. (180–93)

Although, like her literary predecessors, this Jane Shore unquestioningly accepts her guilt, unlike them, she remarks on the curious distinction between standards for men's and women's behaviour; she is guilty of and must pay for a "sin" that in a man would be nothing more than a rather exciting adventure. Like, for example, Churchyard, Rowe paints women as "naturally" more vulnerable to sexual weakness; although this does not extenuate the transgression, it exposes the contingent nature of the morality.

Even more effective as commentary, however, is Rowe's epilogue, which is spoken by the actress playing Shore. The layers of implication here are almost inexhaustible. The actress speaking in defense of a famous courtesan is herself a woman of scandalous reputation merely because of her occupation. No matter how chaste she may be in fact, her professional status makes her fair game for sexual assault and scurrilous libel. Like Jane Shore, she can do nothing to prevent her wholesale condemnation by "good" society, and yet both she and Shore are necessary objects for that society's entertainment. Rowe mocks the audience's hypocrisy and also subtly identifies its surreptitiously erotic attraction to Shore's victimization and subordination:

> What can we say your pardon to obtain?
> This matter here was proved against poor Jane;
> She never once denied it, but in short,
> Whimpered, and cried, "Sweet sir, I'm sorry for't." (6–9)

> There are more ways of wickedness than one.
> If the reforming stage should fall to shaming
> Ill-nature, pride, hypocrisy, and gaming,
> The poets frequently might move compassion,
> And with she-tragedies o'errun the nation. (25–9)

The secret of the success of the aptly-named "she-tragedy" is illicit sexuality, the ultimate desire which may not be satisfied, but which satisfies, to an extent, vicariously. Of course there are no "she-tragedies" about women who gamble, or gossip, or turn up their noses at actresses and kings' concubines; such women are merely annoying, everyday by-products of the cultural resistance/restraint tension. It is in Rowe's play that Jane Shore becomes more than a literary trope of rebellious beauty, parental overindulgence, or the consequences of forced marriage; she performs the function, as do the heroines of Otway and Southerne, of a psycho-sexual catlyst in a society increasingly conscious of the incompatibility of desire and reason.

Desire, asserts Catherine Belsey, is properly the domain of fiction because, after the Enlightenment especially, it comprises "the irrational, arbitrary, inexplicable residue which exceeds or defies the category of the knowable" (11). Until the 18th century, Jane Shore's status as an object of desire is relatively uncomplicated.[2] Rowe's play, with Hastings' amorous assault and Bellmour's lengthy description of Shore's penitential progress, makes explicit the sexual objectification of Shore that is implicit in the earlier accounts. It is this enhanced sexuality, in tension with the increasingly rigid double-standard of the so-called "Age of Reason," that fuels the ambivalence of subsequent accounts of Jane Shore until the more relaxed sexual standards of the late 20th century give rise to another paradigm shift.

In the mid- to late 18th century a proliferation of "historical" accounts of Jane Shore appeared that solemnly proclaimed their authenticity (usually citing More, but also incorporating a good deal of the subsequent popular lore). Morally censorious on one hand, they nevertheless capitalized on the thrill of illicit sexuality even as they dwelt lingeringly on the punishment of the protagonist.

Rowe's play was probably the catalyst. The first accounts appeared in advance publicity for the production (Pedicord xviii–xix). They were cheap (six pence), compact chap-books which became even more popular after the play's success. Such chapbooks continued to sell (still at six pence) well into the 19th century, when editions were published as far away as Edinburgh and Boston. The least embellished of these accounts is *Memoires* (1714), but more enterprising authors from 1708 on cannot resist embroidery. They intersperse these biographical tidbits with quotations or paraphrases of More, scraps of poetry, and other more or less contemporary sources, but these "histories" clearly reflect a distinct difference between their concept of "history" and our own.

These "histories" digress from the classical model of history employed by Thomas More. In the famous "Battle of the Books" of the early 18th century, writers divided more or less into those "ancients" who saw history as a massive, teleological progression toward the present—what has been called the "Whig" version of history (Schmidt 59), and the "moderns," who saw it more as a narrative of lives, and not merely those of princes and generals, but of individuals. This latter position was fueled by the antiquarian movement, which found value in material evidence and philology (Levine 105, 159–62). Unlike true antiquarian undertakings, however, the Jane Shore narratives do not attend to meticulous documentary or philological evidence. Indeed, narrow confinement to "truth"—the antiquarian's ultimate goal, does not characterize them at all. Conversations and inner thoughts are imagined, events interpolated, and the game of literary Post Office makes another round.

Such narratives invited the reader to identify with the protagonist in a more direct way than they might with such Romances as the *Morte D'Arthur* or classically-inspired panoramas like the more recently published *Introduction to the History of England by William Temple* (Levine 166). There are no models in those works for common readers; they have nothing practical to say about the way the world—their world—works. Indeed, these "histories" anticipate the novel in that, like the novel, they "appeal to things on the minds of readers who, while individuals all, share recognizable concerns" (Hunter 93). These concerns are explicitly social and domestic, but they are also implicitly sexual. Jane Shore is of course a moral example—the fallen woman—but she is also a figure of fantasy, at times quite specifically erotic. Hers was not an isolated instance, either. The harlot/heroine paradox, according to Ellen Pollak, possessed great appeal in the early development of the novel, especially, interestingly enough, for women:

> As a female fantasy, the image of helpless, passionate woman seduced, abandoned, and ruined in the eyes of the world dramatized an ultimate nightmare (what always might and often did happen), while it simultaneously offered its reader the vision of an ideal world where she could at once embody passion and innocence, experience forbidden pleasures, and yet retain on record for posterity her essential, if not her social, virtue. (75)

This view is, perhaps, the best explanation for the persistence of Jane Shore's popularity in popular culture, despite that culture's condemnation of transgressive female sexuality.

Though some of the details vary from title to title, and from edition to edition, the narrative is generally consistent along the following lines: Jane Shore is born to a prosperous mercer family called Wainstead (sometimes "Winstead") in Cheapside, London. Her parents are loving and indulgent, perhaps too much so; they lavish every luxury money can buy, including education, on the little girl. As a consequence, she is attracted to high society, and even mingles in court circles as a teenager, where she is greatly admired. This is when she attracts the attention of Lord Hastings (and other courtiers) and becomes the object of their (dishonorable) pursuit. Alarmed by Hastings' attempt to kidnap his daughter, her father sends her to reside with an aunt in Northampton for some months. When she returns to London, however, the trouble begins all over again and her parents decided to marry her off, quickly. The object of their scheme is a wealthy goldsmith, William (or Matthew) Shore. He is usually older (by fourteen years, give or take) than the fifteen-year-old Jane, and quite attracted to her, although her opinion of him ranges from indifference to dislike. She objects to the match, but allows herself to be persuaded, sometimes by parental heavy-handedness, sometimes by rich gifts from her fiancé, sometimes by a combination of both. The wedding comes off, and the goldsmith sets about showing off his new trophy wife.

Lord Hastings, nothing daunted, continues to woo her, paying visits in her husband's absences. On one of these occasions he becomes enflamed and throws her on a bed (or couch), and is only prevented from doing his worst by the lady's screams, which alert the servants. She then complains to her husband, who tells Hastings in no uncertain terms that he is no longer welcome under the Shore roof. Thus rebuffed (one can almost hear him saying "Curses, curses: foiled again!"), Hastings decides that King Edward might succeed where he has failed and alerts the latter to the presence, in Lombard-street, of a very worthwhile candidate for his famous charm. Intrigued, the king disguises himself as a merchant and pays a visit to the goldsmith's shop.

Edward, more subtle than his chancellor, first tackles the husband with shop-talk, and after a time remarks casually that it's too bad there isn't a mistress for this admirable establishment. Master Shore takes the bait and introduces Jane, to whom Edward drinks a toast. He then departs, leaving the husband unaccountably perturbed, and the wife vaguely pleased.

> Edward, back in the palace with Hastings, contemplates his options: To assume himself, and court her in the Character of a King in Lombard-street, he judg'd wou'd be too heinous a lessening of his Majesty; and to force Her from her lawful Husbands Embraces, might be construed such an Act of Tyranny, as would startle and enrage his subjects; obtain her he must, and with her consent, for Love has no charms nor satisfaction in it, except it be mutual and unconstrainid on both sides. (Croxall 185)

To this end, Hastings introduces him to Mrs. Blague (or Blake), a lace-maker and friend of Shore's in whose house the king may encounter and woo her. For some time he remains incognito, and she believes he is simply a charming courtier, if a forward one. In some texts she rebukes Blague for welcoming such a libertine character into her house and allowing him to importune her friend.

The accounts vary some in describing the seduction itself. Several versions have Shore and Blague attending a ball at court, after which Shore receives a letter from Edward, identifying himself. The letter varies in the different versions, but whether flowery or terse the upshot is that "He that can command is willing to entreat" (*History* 10). Alarmed, Shore shows the letter to Blague, who advises her to accept the inevitable, sometimes lying that Edward has already told her he won't take "no" for an answer, and might punish Shore's "sullenness" (*Unfortunate*) and/or suggesting that if disappointed, the king would not hesitate to ruin her husband and her family. By the end of the conversation she has extracted a promise from Shore that she will report to Blague that evening, to be transported to the court.

Shore parts from her husband with sadness, even though in some versions she is secretly attracted to the idea of life at court. She tells him her mother is ill and that she must go tend her. This assures her that there will be no pursuit until it's too late. Blague delivers her charge to the king and then retires, having "lodged this treasure of beauty in her monarch's arms" (*Affecting History* 14). More modest versions draw the curtain with the prosaic statement that, "it being late, Mrs. Blague departed, and they went to bed" (*Life and Transactions* 9). Another, more explicit account, appears in versions *of The History*:

> … and Mrs. Blague, having delivered up this treasure of beauty into her monarch's arms, left them in the temple of Venus to enjoy those mutual blisses they had been so long pursuing.
>   But, O the raptures of that night!
>   What fierce convulsions of delight!
>   How in each other's arms involv'd,
>   They lay confound and dissolv'd!
>   Bodies mingled, sexes blending,
>   Which should most be contending:
>   Darting fierce and flaming kisses,
>   Plunging into boundless blisses. (*History* 13–14)

A brief summary of the remainder of Master Shore's career usually follows: he is heartbroken, of course, and retires abroad (usually after having ruined his business with inattention). He returns to England some time after Edward's death and is last heard of "clipping" coinage in the reign of Henry VII, for which he is executed.

Having thus disposed of Shore's husband, the biographies briefly comment upon her career at court. While they emphasize her kindness and her advocacy, they do not linger on this period. *The Affecting History* (Alnwick edition), for example, devotes a mere two paragraphs out of twenty-four pages to it. Having devoted the first seventeen pages to Shore's upbringing and seduction, the rest of the text concentrates on her downfall.

With Edward dead, Shore is taken under the protection of Lord Hastings. When Richard has him executed (selected accounts reproduce the Tower scene from More in some form), a few of the texts take up the Dorset angle, alleging that Shore remains relatively safe until the Marquis is forced to flee to France. These details, however, are not the burden of the tale, which concentrates on the humiliation and death of Jane Shore. Richard is, predictably, the villain in all these accounts, which also elaborate on the Blague plot: Shore is supposed to have lodged with her friend some of her money and/or jewels against a rainy day after Edward has died. Having been stripped of all her property and forced to do penance by Richard, she appears on Blague's doorstep begging for help. Blague has conveniently "forgotten" that Shore had left anything with her, and chases her from the door. Usually, she is punished along the lines Heywood imagined in Edward IV. Shore then drags herself away to die with, in many of the accounts, a pitiful "Lamentation:"

> Good People,
>   Though, by the rigor of the law you are forbidden to give me any relief, yet you may pity my unhappy state, for the Scripture saith, That to the miserable pity should be shewn. I am now putting a period to a miserable life; a life that I have been long weary of. Nor would I desire to live in the splendour, pomp,and glory of Edward's court. No, I am happier now on the dung-hill, than ever I was in his arms. For, oh! it was an adulterous bed indeed. Oh wretch! that King Edward! that ever I was betrayed by him! What floods of sorrow have my sins occasioned? Oh! learn from me good people, to beware of vain delights; though they promise fair, they leave bitter stings behind them. Alas! you know my punishment is grievous in this world, and so it is, for I have endured a thousand deaths in one; but now, my dying moments are come, I rejoice. Sincere repentance has secured by happiness above. But O, where repentance is not given, what seas of torment rack the soul! O happy dung-hill, how do I embrace thee! From thee my pardoned soul shall soar to heaven, though here I leave this filthy carcase.
>   O that the name of Shore may be an antidote, to stop the poisonous and foul contagion of raging lust for ever. (*Life and Transactions* 13)

Shore's biographers disagree on whether the origin of the name "Shore-ditch" may be traced to the place of her death; some pooh-pooh the notion as romantic nonsense while others assert its authenticity. A brief mention of her parents' deaths from humiliation at their daughter's disgrace is often inserted.

What may we learn from these accounts of the life of Jane Shore? The most obvious development of these texts is their erotic masochism. The seduction material, embellished with the addition of Hastings' attempted kidnapping/rape and the accounts of both Hastings' and Edward's visits to Shore, takes up more than half of the story. The repeated delay is titillating, as is the potential for violence. Real or imagined constraint is present in the account of Shore's capitulation, but unlike Rowe's play, the pamphlets also make much of Edward's charm. The effect is contradictory: on one hand Shore is deprived of agency; on the other, she is more or less content to be forced into Edward's arms ("her lips say no but her eyes say yes"). Once accomplished, however, the seduction ceases to figure; there is little to no discussion of the relationship between Shore and Edward, and the story moves quickly to her persecution after the king's death.

The coda regarding Master Shore is a significant addition, and provides a pointed critique of Edward. *The Unfortunate Concubines*, for example, moralizes thus:

> And tho' this unfortunate Man justly suffer'd at the hand of the Law, in the Reign of King Henry the Seventh [for "gold clipping"], yet it may without any Injustice be said That he was murder'd by King Edward the Fourth, who by enticing away his Wife, brought inevitable ruin and destruction on him and his Family. (122)

The need for "closure" in the account of Master Shore is a prominent feature of these narratives. Croxall raises and then rejects the possibility that Matthew might be the brother of one Richard Shore who became Sheriff of London in 1505 (190). While Shore/Dumont in Rowe's play is a strong, heroic figure, the abandoned husband is more a figure of pity and disgrace in the eyes of subsequent "historians." The loss of his wife almost universally unhinges him, causing him to mis-manage his business until he is ruined. Jane's husband is thus doubly "castrated," in that he fails to prevail, not only sexually and economically, but more important, morally. Accounts in which Master Shore retains his dignity become the exception rather than the rule.

Blague's part in the seduction offers ample opportunity for some misogynistic commentary:

> The Chamberlain knew that Women were the best Instruments to be suborn'd in such Affairs, and that the Sex is most readily betray'd by one another. (Croxall 185)

> O ye fair, be cautious of yourselves, and do not be too communicative to each other, but mark the character well before you are about to impart an affair of much importance, lest, by a precipitate detail of circumstances, you may blast the moment your tongue delivered them. (*The Affecting History* 13)

Blague is a central figure in the 18th-century accounts of seduction, whereas she was a more or less a passive sounding-board in Heywood's *Edward IV*. Her cooperation is enlisted by Hastings, whose desire to ruin Jane in revenge for her refusal of his advances is rather sinister. Nevertheless, Jane takes up with him shortly after Edward's death, although without much enthusiasm, and some writers try to explain the seeming paradox:

> The tongues of men give themselves some license towards an abandoned
> mistress, which she was, perhaps, willing to stop by the protection of that peer;
> or gratitude, as much as policy, might induce her to oblige the man who had
> for so many years retained a constant affection for her. (Croxall 193)

The cumulative opinion of the "historians" regarding the subsequent affair
between Shore and Hastings is that it was the result of the "slippery slope"
effect.

Jane Shore's influence on the king is mixed in these texts, and tends to
follow the ballad tradition. Her concerns are chiefly with "the Poor"; she again
takes on the role of a middle-class Lady Bountiful (*Unfortunate* 127). What is
more pronounced, however, is the explicitly asexual yet "feminine" character
of her influence. Earlier readers of her story would of course have understood
the nature of her power over the king as primarily sexual, particularly given
the metaphoric language used by Churchyard, et al. In these texts, though, it
seems that her role is gently to tease a grouchy king into a better humor. For
example, Croxall says,

> Many times, when Offenders lay under his heavy Displeasure, and the greatest
> Court-Favourites durst not presume to intercede for them; she, with her
> sprightly Wit and pleasant Humour, would so mollify and sweeten the King,
> that many a Man's Life was sav'd, many a Fine remitted, and many a Poor
> Prisoner set at Liberty. (191)

All the accounts are quick to echo More's assertion that she never abused
her power and never sold her favors. None of them, however, ascribe even
the passive agency attributed to her by Rowe in refusing to lobby Hastings
on Richard's behalf against the claims of Edward's sons. Rather, they take
More's line, asserting that Richard's persecution of Jane Shore was on account
of her relationship with Hastings; if Hastings was guilty of treason, then so
must she be.

For the most part, the "historians" see her good deeds during Edward's
reign as evidence of a good heart; there are exceptions, however: note the
vehemence of Sewell on this point:

> I say, tho' all this may be very true, yet there was this Grand Objection against
> every good Work that she did, that it was none of her own, she had no right to
> the Power and Station which enabled her to do it. (19)

Sewell's ire seems to stem not so much from Shore's sexual transgression, as from her social offense in usurping a "Power and Station" to which she was not entitled. He goes on to cite the wrong she had done, and continued to do, to her husband and to the queen. And in his mind her liveliness and wit become positively dirty:

> And, not to mention many more pernicious Consequences of her Lewdness and ill Example, she made vile Return to the Author of her great Beauty and good Wit, by using them as Incentives to Debauchery and prostituting that fair Body to Brutal Lust, wherein Virtue (the best Ornament of the finest Woman) might have shone to great Advantage. (19)

This editorializing is somewhat the more remarkable since it is Sewell who asserts the veracity of his account by specifically citing More as his source; there's certainly nothing in More that would justify such an outburst.

Most of the texts, however, while they damn the sin, stop short of damning the sinner:

> But leaving such Reflections to the Pulpit, I shall rather close her Miseries with Pity, than a galling Censure. It was hard enough upon her that her calamitous Days made up the greater Share of her life. (Croxall 200)

It is perhaps material to note that, while largely sympathetic accounts like *The Unfortunate Concubines* and *The Life and Transactions* went through edition after edition, and were still being reproduced in the 1800s, Sewell's went through only three, in 1714 (Harner, "Jane Shore in Literature" 499–500). Consumers of the Jane Shore story, it is obvious, preferred to side with Rowe: "And since she has dearly paid the sinful score,/ Be kind at last, and pity poor Jane Shore" (Epilogue 37–8).

Who were these "consumers?" They were, obviously, readers, and readers of "popular," six-penny chapbooks. From the description of Shore's merchant origins, it appears that the authors wanted to appeal to an upwardly mobile class of people, but to inject a note of caution as a check to its readers' ambition. It is the Wainsteads' over-indulgence of their daughter with rich clothes and visits to court that begins her descent, often compounded by Master Shore's continuation of that behavior. The biographies thus reflect an emerging capitalist paradox: it is good to aspire, admirable to acquire, but not too much. Prolonged exposure to court life is not good for "decent" women.

These are not mere middle-class morality texts, however. Their continued popularity attests to their entertainment value. One thing that distinguishes them from any previous text is their specifically visual centerpiece, the penitential procession. Certainly, Bellmour's description in Rowe's play invites us to visualize the scene, but we do so second-hand. These texts invite us to become the spectators themselves in a way that More, the original source, did not intend. His description highlights the way Richard's plan to tar Hastings (and Edward) by association with Shore backfired because she bore herself with dignity and her beauty invoked pity rather than scorn. In the 18th century, similarly,

> This publick Pennance of hers at that time being enjoyned her, not so much as a Punishment for her Sins, as to amuse the Minds of the People, that they might not busy themselves about those secret and treasonable Designs that were carring on at Court for the Destruction of the young King and his Brother, and the setting the Crown upon that Monster's Head, which soon after followed. (*Unfortunate* 141)

In addition, however, Jane's beauty itself is a focal point; Richard's motivation is mere background:

> He ordered Jane Shore to be apprehended, stripped of all she had, and do penance by several times walking in a white sheet, and then walk bare-footed and bare-headed in her shift before the procession with a cross and a wax taper in her hand through Cheapside, which she did, looking so lovely in her blushes, that many pitied her. (*History* 14)

This invocation of public penitential would have been largely unfamiliar to 18th-century readers, as opposed to their 16th-century counterparts, for whom public display of discipline was a regular event. The private act of reading invites the reader to participate in the procession, to identify with its focus. To some extent, this parallels the privatization of self-examination and penitence ("closet piety") which emerged in the 18th century, specifically in the rise of Methodism (Hunter 131). There is, however, another element that emerges in these narratives, one of deliberate erotic titillation and deferral of gratification:

> Stripped of all her ornaments, and covered with a white sheet, bare-legged, and the sharp stones wounding her tender feet, she was brought by way of procession, with the cross carried before her, and a wax taper in her hand, from the bishop of London's palace to St. Paul's, through crowds of rabble, who flocked to gaze on her … In all this pageantry of humiliation, she behaved with so much modesty and decent sorrow, that such as regarded her beauty more than her crime, never thought her so fair and lovely as under that

affliction. For, wanting nothing to complete her charms but a little colour, this
publishing of her shame, and the gazing of the multitude upon her, brought
such an agreeable red into her cheeks, as made her look extremely fine. (*The
Affecting History* 21)

There is a kind of erotic excitement invoked by the image of a woman
"stripped," with "bare" head, legs, and feet which the sharp stones "wound."
We wonder what the loose sheet and/or shift might reveal at any moment. *The
Affecting History* is particularly "affecting" in stating outright that it is in fact
her state of humiliation and shame that makes her "extremely fine." Whatever
these texts may say about the undesirability of lust and the transience of beauty,
they also implicate themselves as influenced by both.

The influence of the visual is further heightened by illustration. In the 16th
century, the ballads were often sung to popular tunes, a mnemonic device in a
marginally literate culture (Watt 37–8). In the 18th century, these prose accounts
often had an illustration or two. Illustration further argues the "popular" nature
of the audience. "Scholars" would not bother with illustrations if they expected
their readers to be serious historians; these readers were clearly of a simpler
sort; they were seeking entertainment first, instruction second. Croxall's text
sports an engraving of Shore's penance. *The History* (Boston, 1801 edition)
depicts her on her dunghill, eyes cast heavenward, and an earlier, sympathetic
view of her husband, grieving at her loss.

The illustrations themselves testify to a casual attitude toward historical
accuracy. Sewell's 1714 edition (J. Roberts) is preceded by a frontispiece of
Shore in mid-16th century garb. A pre-dunghill engraving of Shore in *The
History* has her in Tudor court dress. The title-page illustration on the Alnwick
edition of *The Affecting History* cunningly frames her in a bower, wearing a
crown (!), with a male figure with longish hair and an even longer cape kneeling
before her in the foreground, with his back to us. If we need further evidence of
the popular nature of this text there is, appended to the bookseller's name and
location, the inviting, "Where might be had a large Assortment of Histories,
Songs, Pictures, Children's Books, &c." Other editions contemporaneous with
this one actually have elaborate color illustrations. Hodgson's has a fold-out
of Shore begging, with an unfortunate baker trying to sneak some bread to her
past a vigilant guard; The Derby has two: one captioned "an interview with
Lord Hastings," and the second, predictably, "Jane Shore doing penance."

In all, the historicization and pictorialization of "Jane" Shore serves to
contain her within a social context whose aim is to generate eros and then
displace it with pathos. The illustrations work to contain the excitement

generated by the written description, by inscribing Shore in suitably generic and/or repentant positions.

The switch from poetry to prose itself is typical of the Enlightenment, although poetic snatches appear in a number of the prose accounts. The Enlightenment obsession with "knowing" the subject also limits the scope of that subject to what we can know, things like parentage, upbringing, or the etymology of a place in London known as "Shore-ditch." The histories render Shore prosaic rather than poetic; they explain her. While they elaborate on the seduction, they deemphasize whatever pleasure she may have derived from it (while heightening the reader's enjoyment of it), concentrating instead on her penance and misery.

Censorious contemporaries of 18th-century fiction writers often made the argument that such narratives threatened to excite dangerous emotions even as they claimed to contain them. This is certainly true of the Jane Shore narratives, which limit themselves to pursuit and punishment, without any sense of the intervening gratification of desire. They act out the paradox of desire itself: "Past reason hunted, and no sooner had,/ Past reason hated as a swallowed bait/ On purpose laid to make the taker mad." This pattern would characterize the newly-evolving novel as well: It takes Samuel Richardson's *Clarissa* 256 letters of pursuit and deferral before Lovelace's laconic "And now, Belford, I can go no further. The affair is over. Clarissa lives" (883), and any further account of "the affair" is further deferred until letter 314 (1101). While Richardson was criticized for the potentially titillating nature of his text, whatever arousal it might have generated is, in the end, frustrated: it is clear that even Lovelace fails to enjoy his long-deferred conquest, and he is even more frustrated in his attempts to make amends by marrying Clarissa.

In the English Renaissance there is still a place for the erotic in the shared, the public forum of drama and poetry; the mind's eye revels in sensuality even as it exposes its dangerous qualities (see Camille Paglia's discussion of *Spenser's The Faerie Queene*[3]). In the 18th century, however, eros retreats (literally) into the closet. The master and the mistress of a household no longer share a bedroom with their children and servants; and the eye becomes clinical, disinterested, at least on the surface. But the precise descriptiveness of the Jane Shore narratives resists enclosure even as it encloses; to describe is to limit the view, on one hand, but on the other it establishes real presence. Behind the penitent sufferer there is still the woman who defies social and sexual order. She may temporarily be contained by "history," but she is too durable and seductive a creature of imagination to remain so.

Jane à la cour eût un cœur vertueux,

Ah !pardonnez lui sa faiblesse.

Romance 4.ᵉ Partie.

Figure 4.1   Jane Shore in Tudor dress. The French caption translates as "Jane at the court had a heart of great virtue;/ Oh, pardon her weakness."

Figure 4.2   An Interview with Lord Hastings.

Figure 4.3   Jane Shore doing penance.

Vous que sa main se plût à secourir,
Elle est sans pain et sans asile.

Romance 4ᵉ Partie

Figure 4.4 **Jane Shore** *in extremis*. **The French caption translates as "You see, she who's hand was always ready to help others/ Is herself without bread and without shelter."**

Notes

1 See 32.
2 I say "object" pointedly, since sexually, at least, Shore has to wait until the 19th century to experience desire herself. Any "desire" attributed to her in the 16th century is limited to a fondness for gaiety and fine clothes.
3 *Sexual Personae* chapter 6.

Chapter 5

Angel in the House?: or, Jane Shore Domesticated

Nineteenth-century representations of Jane Shore take up where the 18th-century "histories" leave off. This is not surprising given the vast re-printing of the latter texts, which extended well into the following century. During this period, however, the novel, as we've come to think of it, came into being and established itself as a legitimate art form, and the novelistic influence is significantly apparent in an early 19th-century "history" that clearly owes its *information* to the earlier products, but structurally personalizes that information. Lucy Leman Rede's *The Monarch's Mistress* marks an intersection between the Jane Shore story as "history" and as "fiction."

One obvious point to make is that Rede's text is the first purported to be written by a woman. It is unclear whether gender matters here at the level of plot, particularly as so much of the text is derivative. But a striking structural alteration (gender-based or not) has clear implications. Rede's text conveys the story in dialogue as well as in straight narrative, far more so than her 18th-century predecessors. Doing so deepens the psychology of the characters, in particular of the heroine herself, and points toward the inner reflectivity of the full-blown Victorian novel. Eighteenth-century writers told us what she felt, but in Rede's narrative Shore herself tells us. Indeed, there are two narratives in this version: the third-person omniscient one that still pronounces judgment, and the heroine's. In this, the text reaches back to the much earlier first-person narratives of the 16th-century ballads and poems, but the focus is much more on a personal sense of transgression than a transgression against parents, social norms, or social hierarchy.

Rede begins by moralizing; although once in the story we are invited to enjoy the text and revel in its pathos, the initial introduction is severe, using language like "crimes" and "infamy" to describe Shore's career. Having imparted this obligatory censure, however, Rede proceeds along by now familiar lines, to which she adds some inventive embellishments. One particularly startling and amusing flight of fancy occurs early in the story: Shore's previously over-indulgent father has engaged her to Matthew Shore to prevent her ruin by Hastings. On the eve of the marriage, a page disguised as a wedding gift (!) infiltrates the "Winstead" household in order to admit Hastings for a second kidnapping attempt, which is thwarted by Master Shore.

The marriage having taken place, King Edward gains admittance to the Shore household in disguise, garnering an invitation to dinner from the soon-to-be cuckold. Edward employs Mrs. Blague as a go-between, who reveals the identity of the attractive stranger to Jane, and makes her promise to conceal the fact from her husband. Having walked into the trap with her eyes more or less open, however, she complains bitterly when Blague suggests that non-cooperation with the king could have serious consequences for her husband:

> Oh! fate, I am thy victim! if I go not, what would thou do with him? Oh! Shore, I can save thee only by making thee wretched. (19)

Having thus neatly rationalized capitulation, Shore surrenders to "fate" with no apparent dis-ease, prompting the editorial comment,

> Alas for human nature! The mind too soon becomes reconciled to vice, where we love the object;—crime steals on, with slow, but sure steps, every hour adding a link to the thrall, 'till we find ourselves enchained forever. (20)

What is new in Rede's commentary is the implication of Jane's *love*. The passage diffuses the earlier suggestion of coercion and, for the first time, Shore experiences desire; she is not merely an object of others'. This increased tension between the harlot/heroine positions is a result, partly of the increased personalization of the text. When the 18th-century "historians" could remain nominally detached from their "objective" narratives they had less difficulty dealing with the moral ambivalence of their subject. Like Sewell, they could censure her outright, or like Croxall, they could appeal to the historicity of the subject and afford compassion. Rede's decision to analyze Jane Shore's psychology puts her in a narrative bind, especially in the increasingly sexually rigid social parameters of the 19th century. Even her use of "we" as opposed to "one," or "women" in the editorial comment intensifies the conflict; though Rede is recounting a story from history, she is implicating her readers, even herself, in the common human frailties that transcend history.

Like the 18th-century "historians," Rede makes a point of demonstrating how Edward's appropriation of his wife essentially destroys Master Shore. His business goes to pieces, and he is ultimately executed for debasing currency: "… he was the victim of kingly turpitude" (21). While Sewell and some of the other 18th-century writers concentrate on the *institutional* nature of the transgression, i.e., Edward's and Shore's violation of the marriage vow, and the implicit social consequences, Rede emphasizes more the *emotional* betrayal constituted by the adultery. This also looks forward to the Victorian novel, but it would be a mistake to presume that the institutional, social aspect is now absent. Rather, as Tony Tanner asserts, adultery in the 19th century itself represents social dissolution, without having to make that association explicit (17).

Rede's description of Shore's subsequent career is brief, and focuses on her affective power rather than any particular political influence she might have had:

> Years seemed only to increase her influence with the King; and though he had other mistresses, yet she reigned paramount in his affections: whilst her affability, kindness, and charity, made her beloved of the people. (22)

But for her status as an adulteress, Shore here seems like the typical "angel in the house." And although Rede claims she "reigned paramount," the "reign" is limited to *affections*, as opposed to more comprehensive "reigns" posited by some earlier writers.

The rest of the story follows the usual pattern, including a replay of More's tower scene. Following the king's death, Shore reluctantly accepts the protection of Hastings until he, too, is dead, and she is publicly persecuted and deprived of her goods. The penitential procession does not figure as prominently in Rede's text as in the 18th-century accounts, but the familiar themes of Blague's repudiation, the execution of a would-be good samaritan who tries to relieve Jane, and the invocation of "Shoreditch" are all present. Rede also accounts for Jane's continued poverty after Henry VII's accession, based on the animosity of his Queen, Edward's daughter Elizabeth, who would have resented Shore's displacement of her mother. The rest of the text is devoted to reflection. Here Rede attempts to reconcile the ambivalent ethos of her story. First, in dealing with Jane, herself:

> If the soul can be chastened by suffering, and redemption for sins be won by endurance,—surely Jane Shore is forgiven. (31)

The qualifying "if" here, not to mention the passive construction (there is no "we" here), leaves judgment in the hands of others, relieving Rede from having to go too far out on a moral limb. In her justification for telling the story, she is on much firmer ground:

What an awful lesson does the woman's history convey! the proudest prince might pause as he hears it, to think what horrors may spring from his indulging a lawless passion;—and woman, as she weeps over the history must shudder as she marks, that all the derelictions of vice end in misery, in degradation, and infamy. (32)

The pity thus invoked for Shore is again the occasion for a present-day application: this is not just a story of the past, but a cautionary tale for Rede's contemporaries. And (shades of *A Mirror for Magistrates* here) it is not just a warning for women; there is a critique of male desire, too, particularly that of "princes."

Lucy Leman Rede's *The Monarch's Mistress* is a useful bridge between the so-called "histories" of the 18th century, and the novels of the mid- and late nineteenth. The bulk of this chapter will focus on three such novels. They are strikingly different in a number of ways, but they share one central difficulty: how to provoke admiration and pity for a woman who violates that most sacred institution of Victorian England, the family. While "fallen women" are often a feature of the Victorian novel, they raise narrative problems that require substantial—sometimes extreme—containment strategies.[1] The authors, one female and two male, go to remarkable lengths of fancy in order to accomplish this task, and each of the novels reveals a sub-generic variation of the larger novelistic model.

The novel *Jane Shore: or, The Goldsmith's Wife*, attributed to Mrs. Mary Bennett,[2] appeared first, but had a long history of re-publication, serially, and in book form. It was first published prior to the publication of an 1841 edition of her novel *The Gipsy Bride* which notes that it is "by the author of 'Jane Shore,' etc." There are subsequent editions in 1850, a serial edition in conjunction with the periodical *Boys of England* in 1868, and later editions from 1869 into the 1880s, all under the aegis of Edwin John Brett, the editor of *Boys*, *Wedding Bells*, *Something to Read*, and numerous other penny periodical magazines. Although it makes the most of its historical context, this novel is primarily domestic in tone.

James Malcom Rymer's *Jane Shore; or, London in the Reign of Edward IV*, was billed as "An Historical Romance" and published in 1846. Rymer had already established himself as a serial novelist with the likes of "*The Black Monk, Varney the Vampyre*, etc." (title page), so it is at least possible that this text was serialized as well, although it is much shorter, and somewhat less sensational, than *Varney*, and also less episodic.[3] Still, it clearly belongs in a different sub-genre: it is still highly dependent on suspense and action, and flirts now and then with the supernatural.

In some ways the most bizarre of the novels, William Harrison Ainsworth's *The Goldsmith's Wife* appeared first serially in the periodical *Bow Bells*[4] in 1874, and subsequently as a three-decker published by Tinsley Bros. In 1875. *Wife* came late in Ainsworth's career, after his success and popularity had waned considerably, and he was known to have been dissatisfied with the deal Tinsley had offered him, but took it anyway.[5] *Bow Bells*, like *Boys of England*, was a penny paper, and therefore a comedown for the author of *Rookwood*, who had been hailed as a successor of Walter Scott.[6] It is still, however, like Ainsworth's previous work, highly invested in its *historical* quality; there is little either domestic or sensational appeal here.

All three novelists, however, are disciples to some extent of the so-called "Mrs. Radcliffe" school.[7] As Andrew Sanders describes it, books in this school:

> … have a vigorous and straightforward plot, but characters, both fictional and factual, tend to conform to stereotypes, and to be repeated from novel to novel. Plots are molded around historical crises which oblige the novelist to follow a line of development faithful to his sources, but his sub-plots, which are often more involved, show more of a desire for variety than for a complement to the main story. Against a background of historical intrigue, he habitually plays groups of comic low characters, and a melodramatic story of the wooing of a beautiful young heroine by a virtuous and generally aristocratic hero. (Sanders 35)[8]

While we might call Edward's virtue into question, he is nevertheless treated with respect, even with awe, by the authors, and without exception is the most attractive male character in the story; his appeal is only rarely, if ever, qualified.

The three novels share a few other common elements beyond the general plot: Jane is always young, somewhat flighty (to a greater or lesser degree), and always romantically inclined toward Edward. Her husband is always older, described as a "sober" man, and vindictive in varying degrees toward his wayward wife.

All three of the novels portray Jane's marriage in strikingly different manners, however. Bennett's Shore settles down to marriage to the older and rather dull, but doting "Matthew," fairly graciously, despite earlier blandishments from Lord Hastings (who tries to kidnap her) and a mysterious "masquer" (Edward, of course) who intrigues her very much. Bennett also plays some new changes on parental rapacity in the character of Mrs. Wainstead, who is unnaturally ambitious for her child and who encourages her in succumbing to the king's pursuit. Rymer's "William" Shore, on the other hand, is a thoroughly unlikable monster who (among other things) plots the arrest of Jane's true love (Walter, one of her father's apprentices) to get him out of the way and, once married to her, tries to keep her from her father's death-bed. In both these novels, Shore's surrender to the king is long-delayed and much extenuated. Ainsworth's Shore is a little less defensible. Not only is "Alban" Shore a decent, upright, and truly affectionate husband, but Shore herself is restless even before their marriage, confiding rather tactlessly to her fiancé that she would have liked him a lot better had he been a prince (27). Interesting, all three husbands harbor Lancastrian sympathies, a new twist in the evolution of the legend.[9]

The most striking contrast between the novels' strategies of containment (that is, alleviating the harlot/heroine tension) is positioning of the seduction; it takes Ainsworth only seventy-five pages to do what takes Bennett and Rymer each more than two hundred. Bennett's Edward, indeed, orders Matthew Shore's arrest and kidnaps his wife, in Chapter nine taking her against her will to the king's palace at "Eltham" (62). The goldsmith pleads with his wife to be faithful to him as he is hauled away, and she promises to be so "to my last gasp." In no other text have we seen the coercive aspect of the seduction so explicitly expressed. At the same time, the implicit "rape" carries with it a suggestion of its victim's own complicity. For prior to her husband's arrest, Jane appeals to the king's honor in her plea that he not sully hers:

> "Act as a monarch should, and leave me to dwell in peace with him to whom I have plighted my faith!"
> "I will do so—if you declare that you never loved me!"
> Jane's eyes sought the ground, and her blushes increased. (61)

Her lips say no, but her eyes say …

Surprisingly, however, the King does not consummate the seduction immediately. Indeed, the reader learns no more of Mistress Shore until chapter sixteen.

Rymer also employs delaying tactics, concentrating on Hastings' dishonorable pursuit of Shore and only bringing Edward into the picture when Hastings fails to persuade her to relinquish her chastity in exchange for Walter's freedom. Goaded by Hastings, the king makes the usual visit to the goldsmith's in disguise, persuading him to introduce Jane—he's entranced, she's intrigued (252–53).

Both these writers work very hard to extenuate Shore's ultimate surrender. Bennett in particular interposes three years (according to Edward) between

Shore leaving her husband and the consummation of the affair. The moment of truth comes when Edward for a second time thwarts his beloved's attempt to flee his custody:

> There was no way of escape for our heroine. She was conscious that she stood upon the threshold of greatness—that the imperial sceptre of Britain was bowed before her. The arguments of her mother…rushed to her mind together with the fact that it was prophesied at her birth she should live to wear a diadem. It seemed to be her *destiny* to ascend the heights of the earth, that she might scatter blessings beneath her. Reason was bewildered with high thought. She looked on Edward, the first and only possessor of her affections—never came temptation in a more resistless guise—she yielded to the imperative hand which drew her from the saddle and the splendid vehicle received her. (200–1)

This surrender takes place in chapter nineteen (number fifteen in the serialized edition).[10] Bennett has overtly made every effort to extenuate Shore's adultery: she has been badly advised by her mother; she never really loved Matthew Shore, though she remained dutifully faithful long after her removal from his house; she now believes her husband dead;[11] she appears "destined" to succumb; and she is certainly under tremendous constraint. Finally, and this is the ultimate point, she *loves* Edward and always has.

Rymer does not posit such an extended period of time, but he details Hastings' numerous importunities and greatly multiplies Shore's motivations: her unbalanced husband's cruelties, her true love's imprisonment (and ultimate death), and the loss of her father's protection and counsel. Like Bennett, though, Rymer ultimately accomplishes the long-delayed surrender with great dispatch; although Shore makes token resistance at first she is soon overcome:

> Whether it was the sight of a king at her feet, the dazzling splendour of a court, or the irresistible nature of his blandishments, it is not certain; but she relented, and in the end consented. (263).

Rymer very quickly shifts attention away from her for the next four chapters, concentrating on her husband's anguish and furious search for her after discovering her absence.

In contrast, Ainsworth's Shore is a relatively easy catch. All in all, there is minimal attention paid to the pre-Edward career of Shore; Hastings' pursuit is absent in Ainsworth's account. Numbered among her admirers, however, is one Sir Edward de Longespée.[12] Nevertheless, Jane gives her consent to her marriage, which is completed in the next (Book I, chapter 16) chapter. Edward's visit to the goldsmith's shop is the first episode recognizable from the familiar material, but it is not a mere repetition. In fact, Edward has come—as himself, this time—to Alban Shore to borrow money for his invasion of France; his desire to see the goldsmith's wife, though sincere, is secondary. Once introduced, however, the king at once delivers an invitation to "some festivities at Windsor Castle" (45).

Ainsworth, more than Bennett or Rymer, injects a great deal of description, and he is never so much in his element as when he is describing royal pageantry. His account of the Windsor Castle party momentarily diverts us from the goldsmith and his wife. Edward's triumph over the latter is reduced to a casual interlude between episodes of ceremonial pomp:

> Thinking they were entirely alone, Edward addressed a few passionate words to her, and said, "Now, then, sweetheart, I must have your answer. Will you remain here with me?" (70)

Before she can answer, her husband interrupts, and Shore hesitates between the two men.

> "I shall not interpose my authority," said Edward. "Mistress Shore is free to depart if she thinks proper. Do as you please, madam," he added to Jane.
> "Then I will stay," she rejoined. (71)

Ainsworth quickly returns to pageantry, describing a "sumptuous breakfast" given the next morning. The chapter ends a few pages thereafter with the information, "Ere many hours she was installed at the Hunting Lodge" (75).

The potential political impact of the Edward/Shore liaison is vastly different between the novels, once more suggesting distinct sub-generic agendae. The domestic Mrs. Bennett makes it clear that Jane Shore's power is strictly limited: She secures the release of the Welsh musician Leolin, wrongly accused of participation in a Lancastrian plot; and she takes sides against Gloucester and Catesby in pleading for Clarence and Hastings, accused of treason. But the manner in which she pleads betrays the scope of her influence:

> "That hour in which the Duke of Clarence and Lord Hastings die by Edward's order shall be the last which I will spend at court! And the same day will I devote myself to a cloister, never more to quit it! So deal with me, Virgin of heaven, as I keep this vow!" (289)

Bennett does not comment on Edward's acquiescence to this emotional blackmail. And as the outcome is a "good" one (at least in Hastings' case), neither her intervention nor the manner of it is treated as pernicious.

Rymer, on the other hand, seems highly critical of both Hastings and Edward in the pre-seduction period, and for particularly political reasons:

> Engaged as [Hastings] was in political intrigues, he found…that passion for the mercer's daughter would absorb all his faculties, and deprive him of that steadiness of purpose, and real power of action in other affairs, which were so essential to their success. (126)

The King, too, is degraded by his passion:

> How Shore's mouth was to be stopped the royal Edward didn't at that moment stop to inquire, or to settle whether he was to have a pension stuffed down his throat as a recompense, or a pike; but he satisfied his kingly conscience with the passing reflection that Shore's mouth must be stopped. Kingly consciences are generally very easily satisfied; but after all, Edward the Fourth was not the worst monarch that ever ascended the throne of these realms. (187)

The potential violence, public and private, that characterizes the "sensational" novel are evident here. It is in Ainsworth's novel, however, that Shore becomes a fully-fledged political player. Ainsworth actually *emphasizes* that portion of his heroine's life and, further, maximizes Shore's participation in the political matters of Edward's reign. At the same time, he completely elides Shore's sexuality by making her appear, for a significant portion of the novel, as a "young esquire" called "Isidore." Indeed, when "Isidore" first appears in chapter two of book two, "his" true identity is not revealed, and it is not until chapter ten that no less a person than the king of France tricks Shore into revealing herself. "Isidore," continues to function independently of Mistress Shore (complete with male pronouns) periodically throughout the rest of the novel.

Bennett's Shore is praised by the populace for her acts of mercy toward them, and celebrated as having "risen from their ranks to the proud elevation she occupied" (290).[13] Rymer's, in keeping with his somewhat more pronounced political sensitivity, allots her more power, but only in generalizations:

> … Edward never refused her a favour, which is good proof that those she asked, were such as he could grant, and that she never abused her power, for she never took presents or bribes, as others have done.

> Nor was her power bounded by mere acts of mercy and charity towards the poor. Among the courtiers, and on the most important matters, her influence was sought, and often exercised; but never in a bad cause or bad motive. (286)

The conclusion of this first chapter of her "reign" takes care, however to qualify the relationship domestically with "conversation and gentle dalliance," and "love and harmony" (286).

Ainsworth's Shore, however, acquires explicitly *diplomatic* status. Sent as an envoy to the king of France to deliver Edward's terms, "Isidore" acquits "him"self with poise and even a little arrogance. "Isidore" is not infallible, however, for when "Two splendid ladies' dresses" happen to be delivered to "his" apartments, the "young esquire" and "his" attendant just can't resist trying them on, and, presto, change-o!

> "Pardon me, fair lady," said Louis, advancing. "I had all along suspected that the handsome young esquire sent to me by the King of England was no other than the lovely Mistress Shore, and I had, therefore, recourse to this stratagem to elicit the truth." (127)[14]

As implausible as this episode is, it reveals Ainsworth's simultaneous desire to highlight "world-historical" affairs (the objective of the "historical" novelist) without losing focus on the purported subject of his novel.[15] It also poses a remarkable solution for the harlot/heroine paradox, of which more will be said later.

While the novels take very different approaches to the heroine's background, surrender, and influence, they are much in agreement about her plight as Edward's mistress. Regardless of her love for Edward, Jane Shore is haunted by her transgression, in which she, at least, invariably fails to implicate her lover. Bennett's Shore muses on the affair as on an illness:

> Her life with the king had been one long feverish dream, in which the most dismal and horrific phantasmas mingled with voluptuous splendour—the aching of the heart with the proud sense of all but regal power—the torments of remorse with the secret consciousness of beneficence. (325)

Here, Bennett seems to remind us that Shore's sins are, if not justified, rendered less reprehensible, by the fact that she at least didn't *enjoy* them. This reflection occurs close to the end of Edward's life. Rymer's Shore, in accordance with her extenuating circumstances, feels less guilt, though in a far worse condition, having been consigned to Ludgate:

Bitter were her thoughts as she lay in prison; and yet she had not much to accuse herself of, save one heavy crime; but even that was somewhat palliated, when we come to consider that her marriage was not one of her own seeking, and that her husband was every way an unsuitable match for her as regarded age and disposition. (303)

Contrition for Ainsworth's Shore, however, is imposed from without.

Book four begins imagining Shore's and Edward's patronage of William Caxton, who also figures heavily—and equally irrelevantly—in Rymer's story. Rather out of place in Caxton's print shop is a Franciscan monk named "Father Sylvius" who instantly renders Jane uneasy and subsequently reveals himself to be none other than Alban Shore (239). What the erstwhile goldsmith is doing in a printing house, and whether he really is a monk, is not revealed. He delivers a dire, if vague warning to the king that his "time may not be long on earth," which incenses Edward and necessitates Shore's intervention on behalf of her wrathful husband. That very night at a banquet Edward, attended upon by "Isidore," collapses, having been poisoned by Catesby on the instructions of Gloucester (257). Portentously, "Father Sylvius" is present (267) (how did he get in?). He then finds his way, presumably past a host of retainers and followers, to the king's death-bed, where he once more confronts both Shore and Edward.

> "'Tis Alban Shore!" said the king.
> "Ay; 'tis that much-injured man," rejoined the friar. (272)

Alban Shore then proceeds to compare Edward with David and himself with Uriah the Hittite, and when Shore suggests there might be mercy, even for such as Edward, he silences her roundly:

> "Back, woman!" exclaimed [Alban] Shore fiercely. "Thy place is no longer here. Thy days of sinful pleasure are over. Henceforth thou wilt be shunned; for the arm that has shielded thee will soon be powerless, and those who praised thee will revile thee. Vainly wilt thou flee. Thou canst not escape from the punishment that awaits thee. A curse will cling to thee, and hold thee fast!" (272–3)

When Edward feebly objects, the cuckold turns on him:

> "How do I know it?" cried Shore. "Because I have prayed that it may be so, and my prayer will be granted! She whom thou has fed with the

choicest viands, and clothed with the richest attire, will die of starvation, and
almost without rainment! " (273)

Clearly Ainsworth is borrowing here from earlier moral pronouncements
found in the poetry and prose narratives. The comparison between Shore's
court splendor and her future degradation is familiar material going back to
the 16th century. Ainsworth thus again distances Shore from her transgression
by pronouncing the harshest condemnation in the hyperbolic and over-the-top
language of her husband.[16]

The fate of Shore after Edward's death receives short shrift in all the
novels. Bennett introduces the possibility of a liaison with Hastings, and she
redeems it by making it an offer of *marriage*. Although Shore herself would
much rather retreat into religious seclusion, she feels honor bound to give the
matter (concluded between Hastings and the king before the latter's death)
some consideration. Rymer's Shore puts herself under Hastings' protection,
but without the *imprimis* of a wedding ring. Neither author gives Shore much
involvement in the tug-of-war between the queen's party and Gloucester's
in their competition for control of the young king, or in that young king's
subsequent usurpation and disappearance. Ainsworth, however, keeps her
more than marginally involved in the larger political context.

Another important difference between Ainsworth and his predecessors
is the outspoken nature of Shore's *love* for the king. In neither Bennett nor
Rymer do we find the passionate declarations of Jane to Edward that we find
in Ainsworth. Shortly before his death, she cries, "I cannot live without your
majesty," (276), and upon being told of his death she seems about to bear
this out, for she falls ill for more than a week after the funeral. Ainsworth is
unequivocal about her sorrow at the loss of her royal lover:

> Alas! these happy hours were gone—never to return! Deprived of
> him she had so deeply loved, she felt that life would henceforth be a blank;
> and she resolved to bury her woes in a convent, and seek to atone, by penance
> and prayer, for the faults she had committed. (293)

Enter Alban Shore, as if on cue, still in his *persona* as a Franciscan friar. He
informs Shore of Gloucester's successful seizure of power. At this news, Shore
postpones her "retirement" in order once more to serve her country:

> "Hear me, gracious Heaven!" she ejaculated, falling on her knees before a
> crucifix placed on one side of the room. "Grant, I implore Thee, that I may be
> the humble instrument of saving this young prince from the great peril by which
> he is threatened! Grant that my efforts, inspired and directed from above, may

avail to preserve for him his father's crown, which a usurper would snatch from his brow! Grant, O Heavenly Power! that I may be enabled to accomplish this; and when the task I desire to undertake is finished, I hereby solemnly vow to devote the remainder of my life to Thy service!" (296)

Shore's "earnestness and fervor that left no doubt of the sincerity of the supplicant" has a "strong" effect upon the queen, who has serendipitously arrived to overhear her. Elizabeth essentially puts herself in her formal rival's hands, and follows her advice to take Sanctuary immediately. Shore then promises to join the queen and her family, bringing with her what jewels and money she has.

Ainsworth is not content, however, to confine his active heroine to the cloister just yet; she soon leaves Sanctuary in order to work on Lord Hastings, who is only too willing (unfortunately for him) to be instructed by her. Their new-found intimacy sparks jealousy in one Mistress Alice Fordham (analogous to Alicia in Rowe's play), who visits Shore and plants a waxen image of Gloucester in her apartments; this image is used in evidence against her as a witch after Hastings' abrupt demise.

Contrary to the 18th-century accounts, none of the three novels make much of the penitential procession except for Ainsworth's, and his focus is on the pageantry, not on his heroine. Rymer's description of the penitential procession centers more on the crowd reaction than on Jane's feelings, or even appearance. One sympathetic bystander remarks, "The only witchery about her … was her great beauty which has been in this case her ruin" (307).[17] Bennett gives the procession even less attention. This slow phasing-out of the penitential procession's centrality has, I believe, to do with the audience's attitude toward public discipline. Such public displays would have been immediately recognizable to More's readers, since moral correction was a community affair in the 16th century. Not so in the 18th and 19th centuries, when immorality (particularly sexual immorality) became an occasion for isolation of the culprit and expulsion from the social order. The titillating descriptions of the public penance offered by the 18th-century historians (with the visual aid provided by illustration) would have been too overt for 19th-century readers.[18]

Two of the three novels play similar changes on Jane Shore's death; both Bennett and Ainsworth imagine Shore dying in the more-or-less sympathetic arms of her husband. Contrary to the usual run of the story, Rymer does not have his heroine expire immediately. Taking More's lead, he posits her survival for a number of years, eking out a pathetic existence on the fringes of society. Moreover, he appears to derive some moral satisfaction from doing so:

> She had lived a life of penance; it seemed to have been imposed upon her; she could not escape by death from the horrors by which she was surrounded, until her allotted course was run. (318)

While the conclusion of the story thus extends beyond Bosworth Field, Rymer does not give much attention to those political events. It should also be noted that Rymer's Shore expires only fifty-five pages after her surrender to the king. For Rymer, the interest in the story wanes as soon as the pursuit is over; not so for Bennett or Ainsworth. Bennett has a fully-developed secondary plot centering around Leolin, the musician, and the pure Nesta Llewellyn, who functions as a virtuous foil to Shore. By contrast, Ainsworth's foil is "Isidore," and his secondary plot follows the machinations between England, France, and Burgundy which preoccupied Edward in the latter part of his reign.[19]

Jane Shore's sexuality poses a problem for all three novelists: unlike some of the social problem novelists like Mrs. Gaskell (*Ruth*) and Mrs. Henry Wood (*East Lynne*), adultery is not a particular focus for any of them. None of them "do" adultery on a regular basis.[20] Both Bennett and Rymer make their heroine disappear for extended periods of the text: Bennett has her Welsh sub-plot, and Rymer has a huge cast of mysterious secondary characters.[21]

Female sexuality is relatively invisible in both Bennett and Rymer; it is instead displaced onto male characters, most notably *not* Edward, but Hastings and Master Shore. For example, in Bennett's *Jane Shore* Hastings actually bargains with Matthew Shore for his wife's cooperation; he offers the goldsmith substantial compensation if he will surrender his wife. Enraged, the merchant draws upon the courtier, who repulses him with, "I fight but with my peers," prompting the following exclamation:

> Talks he of his peers! The meanest honest servant on his estate is more than his peer! (43)

Hastings then agrees to a duel, in which he easily wounds his opponent, who is thus humiliated. Not for Bennett is Master Shore destined to be the heroic man of the people Rowe created in Shore/Dumont. Here, Hastings is clearly the better "swordsman."

Rymer's deflection of sexuality onto William Shore is even more pronounced. He involves the goldsmith in a double-cross early in the novel, which ends in his being seriously wounded. From that time on, Rymer makes continual references to his loss of "blood" and the way it has marked him in a sinister fashion. At the same time, his mother is identified as having been Venetian (i.e., hot-blooded, sexually volatile) and his heart is described as a "volcano." Taken in context, it is clear that we are meant to see him as both sexually preoccupied and figuratively, if not literally, impotent (71).

Bennett and Rymer also both elide and suggest Shore's sexuality with somewhat gratuitous comments here and there about her. Thus Bennett, in her first description of the post-seduction Shore in chapter 22:

> She was arrayed in a style of splendour suitable to the high station in which she was placed; it might be said however that she exhibited a superabundance of ornament, though so completely did all she wore become her, that such an opinion would not be lightly hazarded. (230)

This passage very neatly subtly critiques the heroine without taking responsibility for it. She is splendid and gorgeous—perhaps a little *too* gorgeous?—but each potential admonition is couched in the passive voice: "… the high station in which she was placed"; "it might be said …"; "… would not be lightly hazarded." Shortly thereafter, Bennett attributes subtle disapproval to Leolin, who

> … desired his wife to remain at present in ignorance of the situation of their benefactress, and determined only to allow her to remain at Tottenham-Court until he should have obtained for her a plain and private lodging elsewhere. (231)

Rymer, in a move instantly recognizable to readers of the 16th-century tradition, early on raises the concern of "dangerous" beauty:

> Jane had the dangerous, often fatal, gift of beauty. Alas! Alas! That the rare endowment, which ought to be a source of much happiness, should almost invariably, in this world of jarring interests and evil passions be productive of much mischief. (81)

Further, he "explains" Shore's transgressiveness by way of other kinds of "transgressions:"

> Jane had been taught the then rare accomplishment of reading. The affection of her fond father had induced him to take that extraordinary step in her education, and to give her an extent of learning which the wives and daughters of many of the highest of the nobility did not aspire to. It was quite a phenomenon for

a boy to be able to read in these "fine old times," but for a girl having such a wonderful heap of scholarship, it was really enough to make a show of. (93)

This commentary (apropos of nothing in particular), also recalls the 16th-century animadversions against over-indulgent parents.

Ainsworth's decision to cross-dress Shore, by contrast, elides female sexuality at the risk of raising the spectre of homosexuality. Such an interpretation, of course, is unlikely to have crossed Ainsworth's conscious mind. Rather, transforming Shore into an attractive page seems to have appealed to his aesthetic and literary sense, recalling Shakespearean heroines' frequent recourse to doublet and hose. It would be naïve, however, given the wealth of scholarship currently evolving about homoerotic desire in Shakespeare and others, to claim that the strategy is devoid of sexual content and/or tension. Clothing itself, notes Valerie Traub, signifies both erotic and social power (119), and the appropriation of male attire by a female, arguably even more sexually and politically marginalized in the 19th than in the 16th century, allows Shore to assert agency in political contexts, thus displacing her particularly *female* transgression (adultery) in a culture where the sexual double-standard was intensely pronounced.

Transgression is transgression, however, and in Ainsworth's novel "it takes one to know one." Ainsworth again seems to reference Shakespeare when "Isidore" bears to Queen Margaret the conditions of her ransom. Once again, although "Isidore" appears quite competent (and is certainly treated as such, given the commissions "he" undertakes), "he" is susceptible to typically "feminine" lapses. Ainsworth's Margaret, like Shakespeare's, is a bitter, prophetic woman who advises "Isidore" to make the most of his "present fortune. Assuredly, thou wilt not have Edward long" (185). "Isidore" immediately goes to pieces, blurting out, "I should die if I lost the king."

> "Die if you lost him?" exclaimed Margaret. "Let me look more narrowly at thee," she added, seizing Isidore's hand. "Tis as I suspected. Thou art a woman! Thou art Edward's beautiful favorite, Jane Shore! Nay, deny it not" (185).

Ainsworth gets quite carried away with Margaret's archaic and heightened speech, which closely resembles Alban's: She announces that Shore will "perish miserably," and speaks to her with "sovereign scorn" (185), "imperious tone," and "energetic gesture" (186), until Shore is quite overcome and departs.

Readers familiar with Margaret of Anjou's history would find the association of the two women quite apt: Margaret's femininity was qualified by her dominance over Henry VI; it was she who led the Lancastrian forces at Tewksbury, not her husband. One dubious female so easily penetrating the male disguise of another dubious female once more foregrounds female transgression and links it specifically to subversion of gender roles.

Finally, while all three novels devote unprecedented attention to Shore's emotional investment in her relationship with Edward—that is, her love for him—they simultaneously deprive that love of erotic connotation, preferring to express sexuality in specifically masculine terms. By blurring Shore's gender identity, however, Ainsworth may have actually heightened the sexual tension. Bennett's and Rymer's Shores transgress sexual norms by leaving their husbands for another man; Ainsworth's Shore, however, actually *becomes* the "other man" in a way. Whereas Edward becomes less and less politically relevant (through indolence and self-indulgence) as the novel goes on, "Isidore," with the exceptions noted above, proves an able courtier, reminiscent of More's Mistress Shore. And while, in female garb Shore is thoroughly domestic, the ease with which she alternates between roles suggests female duplicity, which inevitably has sexual connotations.

Ainsworth's novel, then, most clearly articulates and betrays the harlot/ heroine paradox while failing most noticeably to resolve it. Some explanation for this may be found in the unique situation of Ainsworth, compared to Bennett and Rymer.

Bennett and Rymer had never been considered heirs of Walter Scott. Bennett and Rymer were, at best, popular novelists and they knew it. Rymer, in particular, was an author of "bloods," cheap, sensational stories designed to appear in penny papers. Bennett, while more genteel, certainly, was a prolific commercial writer, as the re-edition and re-publication of her work testifies. Ainsworth, on the other hand, was a self-styled "literary man" whose time had passed, reducing him to something of a joke in literary circles where the social problem novels of Dickens and Gaskell were the vogue, rather than the "historical" and "gothic" novels of the Romantic period.

Sally Mitchell observes that at the end of Ainsworth's career, the "division between mass literature and serious literature grew wider as the number of literate consumers for popular fiction burgeoned … the romantic-historical-Gothic mode continued popular in *Bow Bells* and persisted as a women's escapist form into the 20th century" ("Ainsworth" 47). Even at the end of his career, Ainsworth saw himself as a writer of "serious" literature, even though he was writing for a mass audience. His subject, though, was far from the Walter

Scott-like adventures of his earlier career. Despite his elaborate spinning-out of pomp and pageantry, kings and dukes, Jane Shore's story by this time was inexorably domestic, and thus ill-suited to his purpose.

Much more successful, only a year or so later, was William Gorman Wills' play *Jane Shore*, which thoroughly embraced and celebrated its domesticity. This is only one of the two Jane Shore texts that I have found which actually reunites husband and wife at the end to live "happily ever after." Highly domestic and sentimental, the verse drama enjoyed at least a quarter-century of production, and constituted one of the signature roles of the American actress Genevieve Ward.[22]

The play begins with several aristocratic suitors waiting resentfully on Jane Shore for favors, while Shore herself is occupied caring for the dying King Edward. When Gloster brings news of the king's death, formerly fawning courtiers snub her, and the queen gives orders that she vacate her house. John Grist, a citizen and friend of her husband's, then appears to lead the more-than-willing Jane back to her husband.

It is not as easy as all that, however. "Henry" Shore is sternly opposed to receiving his wife, despite the advocacy of Grist and their housekeeper. Her sin, he says, is one "which finds no expiation—/ The wrong which 'tis debasement to forgive" (27). Jane is distracted, however, by what she thinks is a child's cry—her child's. She begs her husband to bring their son to her, complains that she has sent for word of him time and again and received no answer. In a climactic moment of repudiation, Henry Shore exclaims, "Thy babe?—he's dead!" (30), sending Jane into a dead faint. Her husband then writes her a note upon parchment:

> Great as the sin is, so shalt be thy penance.
> Thy shame be followed by a righteous shame,
> When heaven shall pardon, I will love again! (31)

He then "exits with a wild look at her."

Reluctantly supported by John Grist, Jane goes in search of her husband and forgiveness, only to be overtaken by an order to attend upon Gloster. She obeys, and Grist automatically assumes the worst:

> Ay! That is woman.
> Here is the angel, gentle Mistress Shore,
> Who looketh all around her in the streets
> For expiation from her grievous fault.

When her old pleasures beckon her again,
And seeking expiation from her grief,
Devoutly she doth seek it in her pleasures. (38)

"I perceive a link," he remarks gloomily, "Between all women, be they fiends or angels,/ They are the devil's playthings."

Indeed, it is Gloster's intent to seduce Jane back to the court, but for his own purposes, political and amorous. In an eerie travesty of Shakespeare's *Richard III*, I.ii, he plies his charm to no avail:

> Gloster
> … Reach me thine hand;
> In sooth it is a very white, soft hand,
> Methinks this ring of mine doth suit it well.
>
> Jane
> Your ring, my lord? The loop is all too large,
> As is the homage you affect to me. (42–3)[23]

Unlike Lady Anne, Jane Shore is made of sterner stuff. Goaded by Richard's allegation of the queen's slander against her, she nevertheless draws the line at taking revenge through her rival's children. Her refusal to back Richard's claim of his nephews' illegitimacy prompts him to sentence her to public penance. And although the townspeople, led by Grist, burst in to rescue her, she repulses them, embracing her opportunity for expiation.

Wills does not treat us to the actual penance, just its aftermath. Set at Old Charing Cross in a "Grand snow scene—snow falling" (61), Jane's ordeal stresses pathos and suffering. John Grist, against the pleas of his wife, tries to offer her the forbidden assistance and is savaged by "ruffians." In the nick of time Henry Shore appears to rescue them both.

The final act, once more in the Shore household, brings about the reconciliation between Jane Shore and her husband. Afraid her husband's signs of affection are in fact signs of her own madness, she receives reassurance from Grist:

> 'Tis true, thou has worked out a bitter penance;
> And 'tis as true thy husband rescued thee,
> Pardons, and loves thee; with his love and pardon
> Old home shines up again. (68)

The only thing missing is her child, whom Henry Shore promptly produces, explaining,

> I told thee, Jane, our child was dead, for then
> There was a gulf between thy child and thee;
> But now that thou has battled through the waves,
> And reached the happy headland Innocence,
> Thy child awaits thee. (70)

This apparently complete rehabilitation is without precedent, both in the Jane Shore narrative tradition, and in 19th-century melodrama in general. Whereas T.A. Palmer's *East Lynne* (1874) followed the original course of Mrs. Henry Wood's novel by allowing the fallen heroine only to die in the arms of her forgiving husband (Booth 159), Wills' *Jane Shore* posits a kind of resurrection: Jane's sin is blotted out by her intense suffering and her child—the ultimate symbol of Victorian domesticity—is miraculously restored to life by the all-powerful paterfamilias. And whereas, as Michael Booth notes, the villain in melodrama tends to be the "active principle" (160) who is nevertheless eventually overcome by the forces of good, Wills' newly crowned King Richard fails to get his comeuppance at the hands of dramatic justice. Domestic harmony dominates the conclusion, to the exclusion of all other considerations.

Indeed, despite the differences between the individual 19th-century texts, domesticity dominates. Whereas 18th-century texts dwelt heavily on the cautionary exemplum in the story, a consistent focus both in the novels and Wills' play is the domestic relationships, between Edward and Jane, between Jane and her husband, or both. There is no such coherence in subsequent renditions however; in accordance with our sense of post-modern cultural "fragmentation," the story of Jane Shore will become diffused (and de-fused?) in 20th-century re-presentations.

Notes

[1] See Sally Mitchell, *The Fallen Angel: Chastity, Class and Women's Reading 1835–1880* (Bowling Green: Bowling Green University Popular Press, 1981) for further discussion of the fictional "fallen" woman in 19th-century penny-magazines.

[2] Alternatively attributed to Hannah Maria Jones (Summers 374). However, I have found no extant editions identifying her as author.

[3] See E.F. Bleiler's introduction to the two-volume edition of *Varney the Vampyre* for a discussion of serial-writing in general, and the text itself for evidence as to length, sensationalism, etc. According to Bleiler, authors of serials in penny publications often

wrote open-endedly, extending the adventure until such time as the audience response (or lack thereof) prompted an editor to instruct them to wrap it up (x). *Varney's* length and ending certainly suggest this mode of production, whereas *Jane Shore*, being shorter, and having a finite—that is, historical—"ending," conforms less well to that model.

4   Like *Boys of England*, which published Bennett's *Wife* serially, and *Something to Read*, also published by Brett, *Bow Bells* was "a penny-weekly magazine that featured household advice and needle patterns" (Mitchell, "Ainsworth" 47).

5   Two letters from Ainsworth to Tinsley, 13 Feb. 1873, and 26 May 1875, testify to this tension (Huntington Library). "Ainsworth even had trouble finding good publishers [in his last twenty years]: some of his later novels are so scarce today because they were published in cheap paperback editions by a man called Dicks, in whose penny weekly magazine *Bow Bells* they first appeared" (Worth 21).

6   "Many would have backed Ainsworth's talent against Dickens's in 1840. In the 1860s ... while Dickens was a household name in two or more continents Harrison Ainsworth was antediluvian, a literary joke" (Sutherland 160).

7   Ann Radcliffe (1764–1823) was perhaps the best known of the "Gothic" novelists at the end of the 18th century. Works such as *The Mysteries of Udolpho* were over-the-top historical thrillers, ultimately scorned by more fastidious readers (Jane Austen lampoons *Udolpho* in *Northanger Abbey*.)

8   Sanders is writing specifically about Ainsworth here, but the description applies to both Bennett and Rymer as well.

9   The authors thus revive the larger context of the Wars of the Roses (largely in abeyance in the 18th century), setting Master Shore against Edward not only romantically, but also politically.

10   There are fifty chapters, and thirty numbers in all.

11   Supposedly executed for participating in a Lancastrian rebellion.

12   A rather clumsy *double entendre*, to be sure, but probably the most overt reference to sexuality in the whole novel.

13   Bennett attributes this delicately to "the relation in which she stood to the king."

14   Shore's susceptibility to feminine finery recalls earlier speculations about her motives for surrender.

15   Andrew Sanders notes that "Despite his pretensions to scholarship and didacticism, Ainsworth takes considerable liberties with the facts of history in his novels" (36). All three of the novels slip up (to amusing effect) in this sense at least once: Bennett's Matthew Shore, for example, brandishes a gun (359) during Shore's death-scene, and Rymer's William Shore furiously seizes his hat and coat (282) prior to his departure for France. Such anachronisms continue into the 20th-century novels.

16   Bennett's Shore is confronted soon after her submission to Edward, by "Matthew," who hisses "adulteress!" but otherwise her condemnation is self-inflicted.

17   C.J.S. Thompson later took this remark as the title of *The Witchery of Jane Shore* in 1933.

18   The so-called "sensation" novel of the 19th century should not be confused with some of the more salacious offerings of the previous century. Horace Walpole's *Castle of Otranto* and "Monk" Lewis's *Ambrosio: or, The Monk* certainly influenced such works, but the "respectability" bar had risen. See Wynne 1–22.

19   Ainsworth's treatment of his subject is, perhaps, less satisfying from a conventional point of view than Bennett's and Rymer's. There is no closure of the Richard III story, which seems odd, given the prominence the political backdrop has in the earlier part of the novel.

The latter two include reminders (albeit brief ones) that justice does prevail in the case of Richard III.

[20] Although in Bennett's *The Gipsy Bride*, the reader is led to believe that the heroine has been duped by her lover into a false marriage and that their subsequent child is illegitimate, the marriage turns out to be valid, and the heroine's honor is thus saved.

[21] There is a mysterious magician/trickster named Vasso (sometimes Vassa) who seems to be in the employ of Lord Hastings; a doctor (always referred to as "the leech"); and a character known only as "the faded gallant" who has absolutely nothing to do with the main plot but serves as comic relief. There's also a mysterious "man in grey" who could be Edward but probably isn't; he strikes sparks from his trousers at one point, and goads the goldsmith, with mysterious references to white and red roses, to poison the king. Rymer seems less interested in consistency than effect (see Bleiler xv).

[22] It was also produced as an early silent film which is no longer extant (Harner, "Jane Shore in Literature").

[23] See *Richard* I.ii.204–6.

Chapter 6

"The More We Change …": or, Post Office, contd.

From its inception, the evolution of Jane Shore legend has, for the most part, followed developments in popular culture. Whether audiences were consuming ballads and poetry, drama, prose narrative, or the novel, Jane Shore found her way into the popular *corpus*. As the literate public has increased, so have the avenues of popular entertainment, and Jane Shore has followed along. It is harder, though, to characterize re-presentations of Shore in the 20th century in any holistic manner. Ballads and poetry in the 16th century took either a political or exemplary stance; dramatic re-presentations have steadily shifted their focus from the political to the domestic. Novels, though technically predicated on adultery, have also become essentially domestic, with Jane Shore merely operating at Edward's court as a fairly typical (with the exception of Ainsworth's) "angel in the house." Such domestication continues into the 20th century, but by mid-century social and cinematic developments transform the story once again. It is not possible, however, to establish even a loose consensus among all the texts. Jane Shore re-presentations proliferate more than ever, but their perspectives are highly differentiated. Still, despite different generic and thematic agendae, there are common attributes.

The "Cinderella" principle is prominent in a number of texts, both fiction and non-fiction. The fantasy of the beautiful common woman who entrances a king is archetypal; it is perhaps even more appealing today in a nominally "classless" society in which royalty is still the stuff of myth. Recent historically-oriented scholarship, influenced by Feminism and Cultural Materialism should, by the dictates of common sense, surely run counter to this, but in many ways has become entangled with it with some less than propitious results. Film representations partake of neither convention, actually re-working some of the more symbolic concepts less and less available in linear narratives. One of the most striking developments, however, is the increased sexual frankness and explicitness that begins to appear in the second half of the century; in a culture that no longer has to talk about sex indirectly—one which in fact relishes uninhibited sexual discourse—the harlot/heroine paradigm changes radically. The paradox still exists; we are merely less willing to admit it.

Because of the proliferation of texts, and because of their disparate stances, I propose in this chapter to group them rather arbitrarily. My fundamental argument, however, is that the Jane Shore trope has lost some of its narrative and affective effect at the turn of the 21st century. I would like to suggest why this is so, and what future (if any) there is for subsequent re-presentations. There are three basic groupings: the first is a continuation of the romance-novel genre begun in the 19th century, which becomes increasingly graphic toward the end of the twentieth. The second includes dramatized re-presentations that endow Shore with some remaining symbolic meaning, but with diminishing returns. Finally, there is the "historical" approach, which slowly separates fact from fiction and attempts to recuperate Shore as a significant historical figure.

Not fitting into any of these categories, but too much fun to ignore, is yet another dramatic Jane Shore at the beginning of the 20th century, quite different from Wills'. By the triumvirate of Eugene Morand, Vance Thompson, and Marcel Schwob, *Jane Shore, a Drama in Five Acts* (1901) is a melodramatic *tour-de-force* of hysterical proportions. The text survives only in typescript, and it is not clear whether it was ever performed. In it, the characters threaten to turn into caricatures, as in this speech toward the end by Richard:

> ... Stanley, Bishop Norton [sic]—Hastings! All handsome lords, gay and joyous, brilliant to the eye as this glass I hold in my hand and (*shatters glass*) as easy to break. I will break them. And you—you do not want me to be cruel—You forget that my nature is evil, evil, evil! I was born in pain and torment. I came into the world bloody and deformed, hideous—all hairy with fangs in my mouth—ay, and fingers like the claws of a wild beast. And you have waked the wild beast in me. Now may God protect you! (III.8)

Even Sir Thomas More would fail to recognize this Richard as the king whose reputation he was commissioned to blacken!

One aspect of the play worth noting is the recurrence of constraint as an extenuating circumstance of Shore's adultery. We are told that the king had physically abducted her, and Hobbs (a friend to her husband) notes in the next act,

> She did not yield herself—she was taken by the king. (*looks round*) And when the king takes anything—well, he is the king. Afterwards it came all right—when Shore was dead—for the king is but a man and she a woman. (II.4)

Of course, her husband *isn't* dead, but neither Hobbs nor Jane knows this. This Jane Shore, too, is a political player: as "Lady Shore" she attends to affairs of state with Hastings, she is credited with having caused the king to "settle down" and attend to his duties, and she champions the princes when their father is dead, going so far as to sneak them out of the Tower. In a contrived play-within-a-play scene, she attempts to smuggle them out of the country under cover of a street performance of (appropriately) the Slaughter of the Innocents, Jane playing Rachel ("weeping for her children"). Morand et al. then revert to the traditional ending in which Jane Shore dies in the streets, mourned by her husband, Hobbs, Doll Silk (a prostitute), and Will Spencer, the leader of the players.

By far the most numerous re-presentations of Jane Shore in the 20th century have taken the form of the novel. Since 1905[1] Jane Shore has settled firmly into the historical romance genre. Some authors do try to distance themselves from that genre, surrounding her with "genuine" historical context,[2] but their narratives are rather the history of a legend, not a real woman.[3]

In the first half of the century, the novels' representation of Shore's sexuality remains understated, to say the least. But as early as 1952 it begins to constitute and increasingly important aspect of the narrative. Philip Lindsay's heroine in *The Merry Mistress* is crushed when William Shore fails to consummate their marriage on the wedding night, and she is delighted with her power over him when he finally does. When Edward takes her to his bed, she is nervous that her relative inexperience might put him off and very gratified that it doesn't. In *The King's White Rose* (1988), Susan Appleyard's Jane is even more sexually charged: her enthusiasm makes her husband nervous and impedes his performance. Later, kidnapped and raped by Dorset, she nevertheless enjoys his sexual assault—the so-called "rape saga."[4] The heroine of Arthur Solmssen's *Shore's Wife: A Search* takes great pleasure in "doing it," whether with Edward, Hastings, Dorset, or Thomas Lynom, of whom she remarks he was "surprisingly good at it once one got his courage up, his trousers down" (134).[5] The increasingly graphic nature of the sexuality in the later novels owes much, of course, to the "sexual revolution" of the later 20th century, but its effect is more far-reaching.

In all previous accounts, while the sexual relationships are taken for granted, and sometimes referred to, they have never been described graphically. The later novels' preoccupation with sex tends to make them flatter, less interesting. In earlier literary representations, sexuality always had to be metaphorical, allusive in clever ways. Churchyard employs the "sword" metaphor to describe Shore's transgressive sexuality; the erotic verse that intrudes upon some versions of *The History* sets itself apart from the rest of the prose narrative; Ainsworth foregrounds sexuality by eliding it; even

Philip Lindsay more effectively eroticizes his narrative with descriptions of Jane Shore's baths than with those of her sexual encounters. Once sex takes up any significant part of the narrative, however, the mysterious quality of Shore's power is diminished. Part of what has made her a compelling figure is that her sexuality has always been in the subtext, for the reader to imagine. The very task of writing about sex without writing about it creates a tension that no longer applies when there's nothing to hide. It is that tension which is exciting; this is true about erotic writing in general. It's much more effective to *mean* it than *say* it. The less explicit Jane Shore novels appeal to the "true love" fantasy still with us in Silhouette romances and ads for diamond rings. The sex in Appleyard and Solmssen, however, almost becomes the *raison d'etre* of the novels. The exemplum of Churchyard, the celebration of citizen values in Heywood, and the glorification of a more stately past in Ainsworth are now largely irrelevant.

Sexuality aside, 20th-century novelists take on some other new items of interest in the narrative. Several accounts, following the lead taken by Josephine Tey in *The Daughter of Time*, render Richard more sinned against than sinning, even sympathetic. Gone is the mustache-twirling villain of Shakespeare: the 20th-century Richard is generally much more humane. In her novel *The Goldsmith's Wife* (1950), Jean Plaidy attributes the deaths of the princes to Henry VII, not Richard. Appleyard's Richard (affectionately "Dickon") is overly fastidious rather than evil. In a number of narratives, Richard is genuinely convinced that Jane and Hastings are conspiring against him, and punishes them much more in sorrow than vindictiveness. This recuperation of Richard's character reflects the 20th-century inclination to de-canonize (historically if not ecclesiastically) Sir Thomas More and take his narrative with a healthy dose of salt.[6]

The political significance of Jane Shore varies, and is, in fact, a point of tension, especially when specifically associated with Jane's "feminine" weaknesses. In *The Merry Mistress*, for example, her obsession with Dorset enables him to manipulate her to his own ends: she is so besotted that she agrees to seduce Hastings and recruit him to the Woodville party. Plaidy and Appleyard both spin the romantic tale of Jane rescuing Anne Neville[7] and reuniting her with Richard (in the name of true love, however, not dynastic concerns) and in both Edward takes his beloved severely to task for interfering in affairs of state. In these narratives, sexuality and/or "feminine" intervention is dangerous.

Shore's political contributions are not always treated as injurious, however. In Guy Paget's *The Rose of London* (1934), she is active on both the domestic and political fronts: in the first instance she keeps King Edward on-task when he'd rather be playing, brews him hangover possets and tries to limit his drinking; in the second she coolly plots with Hastings and Stanley to assassinate Richard to prevent him from seizing the throne (244).[8] And Solmssen's heroine (when she isn't "doing it") is privy to the other chief actors' confidences, and it is she who comes up with many of the strategies then carried out by Hastings, Lynom, and even Bishop Morton.

The novelists are not always particularly sensitive to historical accuracy. Lindsay's heroine takes an astonishing number of baths for a medieval woman. The female prisoners in Appleyard's Ludgate live in dormitory-like cells with beds in them. Solmssen's Jane, Hastings and Bishop Morton share a cozy breakfast of eggs and milk.[9] The novels also vary in their conclusions more than in the previous re-presentations. In *The Rose of London* Jane lives to a ripe old age, happily wedded to Thomas Lynom. Lindsey's novel ends with the promise of the marriage. Plaidy's Jane expires, a "little old beggar-woman" (314). Appleyard's Jane Shore graciously refuses Lynom's offer of marriage, and the novel ends with her leaving Ludgate Prison, off, presumably, to "fresh woods and pastures new."

One would like neatly to trace an evolving political agency for Shore, paralleling the evolution, in the 20th century, of women's rights. Alas, this does not seem possible; the novels that minimize her agency are not confined to the pre-women's movement years. I would argue that the choice of whether or not to empower Shore politically had more to do with the sub-genre of the text, and the intended audience. Appleyard's *White Rose*, as the cover art attests, is essentially a "bodice ripper." Such texts tend to favor victimized heroines in thrall to strong men, even though they may, in the end, become "winners" (Thurston 219, n.2). Solmssen's Shore, the most "contemporary" of all, nevertheless ends up pregnant (if not barefoot), and her political machinations are all indirect; she provides the ideas, but men carry them out.

Although Shore's symbolic status as a figure representative of social instability seems to recede in the novels, it interestingly reasserts itself other genres, both when she is foregrounded and when she is elided. As film has succeeded stage, so have there been cinematic Jane Shores. The early ones work along more or less the same lines as previous representations, and for good reason. The earliest script was based on Rowe (1911), and two subsequent films (1915 and 1922) were amalgamations of Rowe and Wills (Harner, "Jane Shore in Literature" 505). Neither of these films is extant, but Shakespeare's *Richard III* is still with us, and when Laurence Olivier produced his version in 1955 he actually wrote in a part for Jane Shore. She has no lines, but she appears in the flesh as a mysterious odalisque at key points in the action.

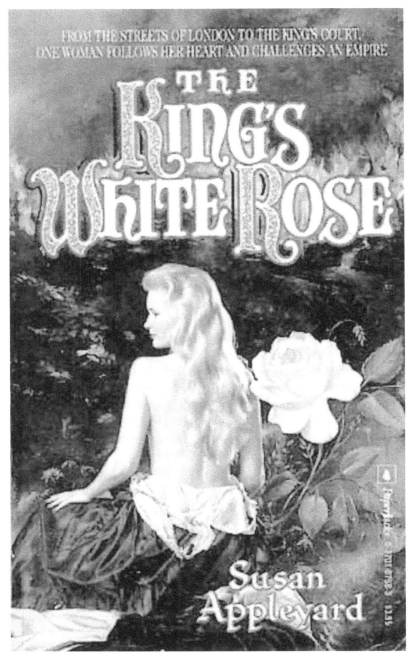

Figure 6.1 **Cover art for Susan Appleyard's** *The King's White Rose*.

Played by Pamela Brown, she is a stark contrast to Mary Kerridge as Edward's queen: Brown is costumed with a plunging neckline and flowing headdress; Kerridge seems confined by her clothing like a tightly wrapped package and her severe headdress puts one in mind of a helmet.

Olivier clearly considered seriously his placement of Shore. She appears in the first scene, foregrounded, smiling knowingly, as Edward is crowned. She is present, giving Edward a drink just as he signs the death warrant for Clarence. She is also present when Richard intercepts Clarence's pardon, at the ill-fated reconciliation between Hastings and the Queen's faction, and in bed with Hastings when Stanley's messenger delivers his master's premonitory dream, which Hastings, of course, laughs off. Finally, she warmly kisses him goodbye *en deshabille* soon after Hastings has flatly refused Catesby's suggestion that Richard become king. The cumulative effect is unmistakable: Jane Shore may not *be* death, but she is inextricably associated with it.

Olivier further conveys this impression in his direction of speeches. The ribald exchange about Shore takes place in her presence, as she personally delivers Hastings from the Tower, and in subsequent discussion of Edward's illness, Olivier directs the line, "O, he hath kept an evil diet long/ And overmuch consum'd his royal person" (I.i.139–40) specifically at her. In the above-mentioned reconciliation scene, while declaring his love of, "Dukes, earls, lords, gentlemen—indeed of all" (II.ii.69) he aims the pause at her, as if to call attention to the dubious justice of her presence at such a time. Finally, as the lords follow Richard from the Tower, leaving Hastings to the hands of Catesby and co., Buckingham's line, "I never looked for better at his hands/ After he once fell in with mistress Shore" (III.v.50–51) is delivered ponderously, complete with close-up. Without doubt, Olivier not-so-subtly transformed his odalisque into a basilisk.

Jane Howell, who directed the BBC/Time-Life video production in 1982 may have had Olivier in mind when she adopted a supernumerary Shore, but gave her no such powerful symbolic effect. Played by Anne Carroll, she turns up only once, to bid Hastings goodbye as he leaves for the Tower; she appears on Catesby's line, "'Tis a vile thing to die, my lord,/ When men are unprepar'd and look not for it (III.ii.62–3) and Hastings references her briefly with a kiss when he speaks the line, "I hold my life as dear as you do yours,/ And never in my days, I do protest,/ Was it so precious to me as 'tis now" (78–80). She lingers in the background until Catesby's exit with Stanley, and that is all we ever see of her.

In contrast, Jane Shore is conspicuously *absent* in the 1995 Richard Loncraine/Ian McKellan film, which relocates the action to a circa-1930s,

Figure 6.2   Pamela Brown as Jane Shore in Olivier's *Richard III* (Criterion/Janus).

pseudo-fascistic Britain. Any reference to her is cut from the script, which instead sentimentally emphasizes the relationship between the older and already ailing King Edward (John Wood) and his queen (Annette Bening). Bening, indeed, becomes the heroic focus, especially in Shakespeare's Act IV, scene iv, when the queen and Richard hurl words like weapons at each other in a final struggle for ascendancy. Olivier cut this scene, further marginalizing the queen in his production. Loncraine and McKellan, however, play it to the hilt, emphasizing Richard's kinky, over-the-top sexuality (he virtually sexually assaults the queen at the same time he is trying to persuade her to let him marry her daughter). Olivier's interpretation rendered female beauty and sexuality dangerous (Jane Shore) and susceptible (Lady Anne); Loncraine and McKellan contrast the perverted sexuality of Richard with the purity of Richmond and Princess Elizabeth who awake in each others' arms the morning after their stolen wedding, naked, flushed and gleaming. In this universe of stark black and white, evil and good, there is no place for Jane Shore, harlot *and* heroine.

There is no doubt some contextual basis for the contrast between the 1955 and 1995 versions. Olivier could afford the nudge-nudge/wink-wink sexual humor and death symbolism surrounding Mistress Shore when England was innocently celebrating post-WWII reconstruction in the reign of a handsome young queen with her handsome young family. But there is a wistful touch of paradise lost in the relationship between the king and queen in 1995; a nostalgia for the loving royal family even in the face of illness and treachery. In the wake of shattered Windsor marriages, royal infidelity was neither funny nor symbolic of something else. Such distaste, if only suggested by elision, is evident in a recent historical account.

Since the 1970s, beginning with the work of Nicholas Barker, there has been renewed interest in identifying and tracing the life of the "real" Jane Shore. The most recent and thorough manifestation is Desmond Seward's account in *The Wars of the Roses: Through the Lives of Five Men and Women of the Fifteenth Century* (1996). But the attitude of the 20th-century historian toward Shore is not, in fact that much different from that of the 18th-century "historian." In explaining his choice of subjects, Seward remarks,

> I would have liked to have included someone from "the wrong side of the tracks," but sadly the period has left too little documentation about common folk, so I have had to make do with the harlot. (13)

By "the wrong side of the tracks," then, Seward means to indicate a social, rather than moral distinction. But of course Jane Shore was indeed socially distinct from "a squire and a nobleman … a great lady, [and] a priest" (13). Somehow, then, her status as "harlot" seems to make her less worthy as a historical subject. Why? We seem to have come full circle back to More's concern that Shore may be thought "to sleight a thing" to figure in the history of great events. Nevertheless, Seward must "make do" with her if he wants to conform to our growing interest in the lives of ordinary people in history, so she is here.

Or rather, her *father* is here. Seward actually writes a great deal more about John Lambert, mercer of London, than about his daughter Elizabeth, a.k.a. "Jane." Indeed, little of Seward's material on Elizabeth Shore goes beyond what Barker discovered in the '70s. In order to say anything new, then, Seward had to delve into the career and transactions of Master Lambert, as well as those of William Shore. So Seward gets his "common folk," after all, with only the slight regret that they are tainted by their association with a "harlot."

As Seward himself admits, "our knowledge of Jane Shore and of her relations with King Edward IV is very scanty indeed" (231). The earliest historical reference he can find to her is her petition to annul the marriage to William Shore. Prior to this, he has only been able to speculate about what "may" have transpired through references to Thomas More, and city records concerning her father. Like Barker before him, Seward questions whether the charge of impotence was actually true; it was, according to Seward, an "apparently unique" case in its time (230). And the petition was not granted easily; an appeal had to be made to the Pope before the annulment was approved, and this would have been expensive. Still, there is no evidence extant to involve Edward in the final settlement; indeed, Shore's marital status would have been irrelevant to him, since he was himself married and in any case would not have married a mercer's daughter if he wasn't.

Unlike More and the authors who followed him, Seward says next to nothing about Shore's reputed generosity and advocacy during her tenure as Edward's concubine. He does, however, take on trust the tradition that Shore reverted to the protection of Lord Hastings after Edward's death. He also accepts without question that she had a relationship with Dorset. Indeed, he rather romantically embellishes it:

> The obvious person for the Marquess to run to was Mrs. Shore; someone as kind as Jane would never turn him away. In any case, he was in love with her, and he had been without a woman at Westminster. It is quite possible, therefore, that she was arrested for sheltering Dorset. Undoubtedly they were together later that year, during the summer or in the early autumn. (268)

Seward's only evidence for this astonishingly positive ("Undoubtably ...") pronouncement is, of course, the writ of attainder against Dorset. Richard being the propagandist that he was, however, I am not at all convinced, as I suggested earlier, that Shore's inclusion in the proclamation against Dorset was not merely additional window-dressing: a further nail in the coffin of Dorset's reputation.[10] I can, without further evidence, do no more than speculate, and I hesitate to speak with Seward's certainty. How he knows for sure that Dorset was "in love" with Shore, he does not say.

Richard's letter to Bishop Russell, lamenting his solicitor Thomas Lynom's engagement to Shore signals a return to documentary research for Seward as opposed to speculation. He traces Lynom's career briefly, describing him as one of "a new breed of specialist bureaucrat which entered the royal service during the Yorkist period" (286). Seward suggests that "Mrs. Lynom's second marriage must have been overshadowed, not so much by the burden of an unaccustomed respectability as by the problems of her husband's employer" (288). The note of sarcastic prudery ("unaccustomed respectability") seems inappropriately Victorian for a post-modern historian, but it is of a piece with Seward's thinly veiled contempt.

The last documents specifically to name Shore are the wills of her parents. In addition to a "bed of arras" her father left her "'a stained cloth of Mary Magdalen and Martha.'" Seward then coyly speculates: "(Did John have his tongue in his cheek, leaving his daughter a marital bed with a picture of the repentant Magdalen?)" (341). This additional parenthetical dig is followed by a rather complacent acceptance of the More version of Shore's aging and death:

> Having lost Mr. Lynom, she found herself an old woman, ugly and penniless, no longer capable of attracting protectors. More, writing no earlier than 1518, paints a harrowing picture of Jane as she had become by then—"lean, withered and dried up, nothing left but raveled skin and hard bone." (343)

Dismissing any suggestions that her plight might not have been so bad, and that More was rather trying to craft a rhetorical argument than a strictly historical account, Seward concludes, "The bleakest interpretation is probably closest to the truth. She begged her bread miserably through the streets of London" (343).

What is notable and mystifying about Seward's account of Jane Shore is the almost palpable hostility and distaste implied by his language throughout. Language is not value-neutral, and Seward's account of Jane Shore is loaded with sneers and jibes. From his introduction apologizing for having to "make do" with a "harlot," to his confident assertion that she begged "miserably," Jane Shore is once more in the pillory.

Containment and reinscription—functions of Jane Shore re-presentations from then to now—still seem to be at work. Death is no longer a required fate for the adulteress, but she still is subject to the conscious or unconscious attraction/ambivalence of her "handler." What does this say about us, about a culture that *seems* so permissive, and yet still harbors its throwbacks?

Conclusion

I have observed the misapprehension—among college students, at least, but also among others who should know better—that the further back one goes in history, the more prudish and socially conservative the society. The saga of the Jane Shore story proves that to be untrue at a glance. Adultery in high places has really only recently become a *political* liability in the Anglo-American ethos.[11] The gleeful ribaldry of Chaucer's *Canterbury Tales*, Rabelais' *fabliaux*, and Shakespeare's plays remind us that our medieval and early modern ancestors were much more matter-of-fact than we about the body and its various functions. Though we consider ourselves much more "liberated" now, with sex education in schools and condom machines in tavern bathrooms, our attitude toward sex has become at once more complicated and more trivialized. We have not, then, abandoned narrative symbolism, and we still apply it to so-called "real life," not only as Seward does in the case of Jane Shore, but in our own contemporary self-narratives.

Take, for instance, the Starr Report. James Woods draws an interesting parallel between this "objective" account and the 19th-century adultery novels examined by Tony Tanner. Woods observes that it "is not a neutral legal account but a literary confection, dusted with detail" (16). Why, for example, asks Woods, is it important to note that one of Clinton's sexual encounters with Lewinsky took place "on Easter Sunday, April 7, 1996" (17)? The date itself may or may not be relevant, but the psychological one-two delivered by *Easter*, a holy day, a family day, was too good to pass up. Just like Seward, Starr uses "loaded" language to "document" an affair in high places. Similarly, the woman in the case bears the brunt of the linguistic ridicule,[12] even if the primary purport of the document is, like More's, to discredit the derelict leader.

Woods concludes:

The nineteenth-century novel of adultery, on which Starr's report is so parasitic, achieves its greatness through a tension: on the one hand, it believes in and upholds the law, and generally punishes its amorous malefactors with death and disgrace. On the other hand, it has a sympathy with its lovers, with their banality and hot wrongdoings, which works to subvert the very upholding of the law. (17)

The appeal of "romance," to use novelist Muddock's term, is still with is, even when—perhaps especially when—romance collides with order.

Whither Jane Shore next, then? Although the re-presentations considered in this study have clearly drawn on their own circumstances of production for details, this four-century game of Post Office seems remarkably durable. While topical sex scandals will come and go (does anybody know what even happened to Monica Lewinsky?), they are dependent for their representation on a huge social/political psychology which the Shore legend establishes as culturally embedded. If, as Helgerson has stated, the story of the Jane Shore saga is the story of the development of our own literary self-representation (34), we have changed very little since 1517.

Historically, Elizabeth Lambert Shore (Lynom) has achieved a focus she would probably never have attained if she had not been the heroine of popular literature. As such she remains emblematic of our culture's deep-rooted ambivalence about what it sees as "illicit" sexuality that threatens social order both as a violation of conventional morality and as an instrument of unauthorized political influence. And as long as these anxieties seek containment in linguistic and narrative strategies the harlot/heroine archetype will figure in our quest for coherent narrative self-representation.

Notes

[1] The publication date of *Jane Shore A Romance of History* by J.E. (Joyce Emerson) Preston Muddock (London: John Long). Very similar to Rymer's novel except in the treatment of "Matthew" Shore, whom Muddock renders heroic, despite his Lancastrian sympathies. In her conclusion, as in Wills', husband and wife are reconciled and reunited, and when her husband dies, Jane enters a nunnery.

[2] See, for example, C.J.S. Thompson, *The Witchery of Jane Shore* (London: Grayson and Grayson, 1933).

[3] A late-emerging feature in the popular texts is the anecdote about Shore saving Eton College from bankruptcy in Edward IV's time (see Birley 408); there are even portraits identified as hers at the College today (409).

[4] See Thurston, 78–9. I would like, however, to go on record that I do not share her ultimately benign interpretation of such narratives.

Figure 6.3   **"Starr-Crossed Love" by Vint Lawrence (used by permission)** *The New Republic* **5 October 1998.**

5   What a 15th-century solicitor is doing wearing "trousers" I cannot imagine. Later, Solmssen gives Jane a completely gratuitous sexually explicit dream for good measure.

6   This is not to say that history has completely exonerated Richard. Charles Ross, for instance, argues that it is perfectly plausible that Richard murdered his nephews (*Richard* 98–104).

7   This is the Lady Anne formerly married to Edward VI's son, daughter of the "Kingmaker" Warwick. Upon her father's death, the Dukes of Clarence and Gloucester quarreled bitterly over her (or rather her lands). There is a legend that Clarence kidnapped the girl (his wife's sister) and placed her in service in a London household, where she was finally discovered and removed by Richard. The two, sincerely in love, married, thereby frustrating Clarence's hopes of keeping her wealth in his own control.

8   Paget also includes the Anne Neville story, *without* Edward's criticism.

9   Considering that Solmssen, himself a lawyer, has woven his narrative scrupulously around all of the extant documents regarding Shore (her father's will, the chronicle accounts, Richard's letter to the Bishop of London, etc.), it is somewhat mystifying that he commits such blatant anachronistic howlers as serving Sir William Stonor scrambled eggs for breakfast and having Jane carry a handkerchief in Ludgate prison.

10   Seward himself notes that Shore enjoyed "star billing in the propaganda that followed" Hastings' execution. "She was going to be attacked publicly by Buckingham and she would also feature in a further proclamation. The régime was trying to make her the symbol of its opponents' 'vicious living'" (270). Later he asserts again that Shore was a "key exhibit in [Richard's] smear campaign" (273).

11   Samuel M. Pratt, in "Jane Shore and the Elizabethans," speaking of her initial incarnation in More, reminds us of the cultural differences which separate us from the late 15th century:

> When the reader thinks of More in one of his roles, the unworldly man who wore a hairshirt and whipped his body, he may find More's acceptance, his actual approval of Jane Shore hard to credit. If one expects moral condemnation from the man who was eventually canonized, he is surprised by More's account. The explanation of this surprise, I suggest, lies in a view alien to the 20th century. The reader of More will have difficulty escaping the conclusion that More granted a king the right to have a mistress. (1294)

12   "… in narrative terms, the president must be both stripped of his office and yet retain enough prestige that the idea of dereliction still has force; thus, Clinton is called only 'the president' throughout." And, although Monica's "vagina" is mentioned several times, the president only ever has 'genitals' (17).

Bibliography

Primary Texts

"The Affecting History of Jane Shore, Concubine to King Edward IV. Giving An Account of her Birth and Parentage, Her Marriage with Mr. Shore, a Goldsmith, in London, Her Seduction by the King, Her great Wretchedness and Misery after the King's death, and her deplorable End in a Ditch." Alnwick: W. Davison, 1830.

Churchyard, Thomas."Howe Shores wife, Edwarde the fowerthes concubine, was by king Richarde despoyled of all her goodes, and forced to do open penance." *The Mirror for Magistrates*. Ed. Lily B. Campbell. New York: Barnes & Noble, 1938.

Chute, Anthony. "Bewtie dishonoured, written under the title of Shores Wife." London: Imprinted by John Wolfe, 1593.

Deloney, Thomas. "A New Sonnet containing the Lamentation of Shores wife, who was sometime Concubine to King Edward the fourth, setting forth her great fall, and withall her most miserable and wretched end." The Garland of Good Will: Early English Poetry, Ballands and Popular Literature of the Middle Ages v. XXX. London: Printed for the Percy Society, 1852.

Drayton, Michael. *Works* v. 2. Ed. J. William Hebel. Oxford: Basil Blackwell, 1961.

Heywood, Thomas. *First and Second Parts of King Edward IV*. The Dramatic Works of Thomas Heywood, v. 1. New York: Russell and Russell, 1964.

"The History of Jane Shore." In Samuel *Croxall's A Select Collection of Novels and Histories*, v. iii. 2nd edition. London: J. Watts, 1729: 165–200.

"The History of Jane Shore, Concubine to King Edward IV. Giving an Account of her Birth, Parentage, Her Marriage with Mr. Matthew Shore, a Goldsmith, in Lombard-street, London. How She Left Her Husband's Bed to Live with King Edward IV. And of the Miserable End She Made at Her Death." Boston: Printed near Charles-River Bridge, 1801.

"King Edward IV and the Tanner of Tamworth." Illustrated British Ballads v. 1. Ed. George Barnett Smith. Cassell, Peter, Galpin & Co., 1881: 199–202.

"The Life and Transactions of Mrs. Jane Shore, Concubine to King Edward IV. Containing an Account of Her Parentage, Wit and Beauty, Her Marriage with Mr. Shore. The King's Visits to Her, Her Going to Court, and Leaving her Husband. Her Great Distress and Misery after the King's Death, &c." Glasgow: Printed for the Booksellers, 1828.

Lindsay, Philip. *The Merry Mistress*. New York: Roy Publishers, 1952.

Memoires of the Lives of King Edward IV and Jane Shore. Extracted from the Best Historians. London: E. Curll, 1714.

Morand, Eugene, Vance Thompson, and Marcel Schwob. *Jane Shore, a Drama in Five Acts* (1901).

More, Thomas. "History of King Richard III" [Historia Richardi Regis Angliae Eius Nominis Tertii]. *The Complete Works of St. Thomas More* v. 2. Ed. Richard S. Sylvester. New Haven: Yale University Press, 1963.

_____. "The Best State of a Commonwealth and the New Island of Utopia." *The Complete Works of St. Thomas More*, v. 4. Richard S. Sylvester, executive ed. New Haven: Yale University Press, 1965.

Muddock, J.E. Preston. *Jane Shore: A Romance of History.* London: John Long, 1905.

Padget, Guy. *The Rose of London.* London: Hutchinson & Co., 1934.

Plaidy, Jean. *The Goldsmith's Wife.* New York: Putnam & Sons, 1950.

Richard III. Dir., Laurence Olivier. With Laurence Olivier, Cedric Hardwicke, Ralph Richardson, John Gielgud, and Claire Bloom. Janus Films, 1955.

Richardson, Samuel. *Clarissa: or, the History of a Young Lady.* Ed. and with introduction and notes by Angus Ross. New York: Penguin, 1985.

Rowe, Nicholas. *The Tragedy of Jane Shore.* Ed. Harry William Pedicord. Regents Restoration Drama Series, John Loftis, General Ed. Lincoln: Nebraska University Press, 1974.

Sewell, George [?]. "The Life and Character of Jane Shore. Collected from Our Best Historians, Chiefly from the Writings of Sir Thomas More; Who Was Her Cotemporary, and Personally Knew Her. Humbly Offer'd to the Readers and Spectators of Her Tragedy Written by Mr. Rowe. Inscrib'd to Mrs. Oldfield." London: J. Morphew and A. Dodd, 1714.

Shakespeare, William. *The Tragedy of Richard III. The Complete Works of Shakespeare*, Fourth Ed. Ed. David Bevington. New York: HarperCollins, 1992.

"The Stonor Letters and Papers, 1290–1483," v.2 (Royal Historical Society). Charles Lethbridge Kingsford, Ed. *Camden Society* ser. 3. London, 1919.

Thompson, C.J.S. *The Witchery of Jane Shore.* London: Grayson and Grayson, 1933.

"The Unfortunate Concubines: The History of Fair Rosamond, Mistress to Henry II; and Jane Shore, Concubine to Edward IV; Kings of England. Shewing How They Came to Be So. With Their Lives, Remarkable Actions, and Unhappy Ends." London: T. Norris, 1717.

Wills, W.G. *Jane Shore.* London: Tinsley Brothers, 1876.

"The Woefull Lamentation of Mrs. Jane Shore, a Gold-smith's Wife of London, who for her Wanton Life came to a Miserable end. Set forth for the Example of all Wicked [lewd] Livers*." The Roxburge Ballads* v. 1. William Chappell, ed. Hertford: Steven Austin and Sons, 1888.

Secondary Texts

Aikins, Janet E. "To know Jane Shore, 'think on all time backward.'" *PLL* 18:3 (1982): 258–77.

Baines, Barbara J. *Thomas Heywood.* Boston: Twayne Publishers, 1984.

Barker, Nicholas. "The Real Jane Shore." *Etoniana* (June 4, 1972): 391–97.

Beith-Halahmi, *Esther. Angell Fayre or Strumpet Lewd: Jane Shore as an Example of Erring Beauty in Sixteenth-Century Literature. Elizabethan and Renaissance Studies* 26. Salzburg Studies in English Literature, James Hogg, ed. 1964.

Belsey, Catherine. *Desire: Love Stories in Western Culture.* Oxford: Blackwell Publishers, 1994.

Birley, Sir Robert. "Jane Shore and Eton." *Etoniana* (December 2, 1972): 409–10.

Bleiler, E.F. Introduction to *Varney the Vampyre: or, The Feast of Blood* by James Malcom Rymer or Thomas Pecket Prest. New York: Dover Publications, Inc., 1972–73.

Booth, Michael R. *Theatre in the Victorian Age.* Cambridge: Cambridge University Press, 1991.

Born-Lechleitner, Ilse. *The Motif of Adultery in Elizabethan, Jacobean, and Caroline Tragedy.* Saltzberg Studies in English Literature, James Hogg, ed. New York: Mellen Press, 1995.

Coleman, Janet. *Medieval Readers and Writers 1350–1400.* New York: Columbia University Press, 1981.

Dean, Leonard F. "Literary Problems in Richard III." *PMLA* (1943): 22–41.

Freud, Sigmund. *Civilization and its Discontents.* Translated and edited by James Strachey. New York: WW Norton, 1961.

_____. *Sexuality and the Psychology of Love.* Edited by Philip Rieff. New York: Collier Books, 1963.

Gouge, William. *Of Domesticall Duties.* London, 1622.

Guy, John. "The 1590s: the Second Reign of Elizabeth I?" *The Reign of Elizabeth I: Court and Culture in the Last Decade.* John Guy, ed. Cambridge: Cambridge UP, 1995: 1–19.

Harner, James L. "Jane Shore in Literature: A Checklist." *Notes & Queries* 28 (December 1981): 496–507.

Helgerson, Richard. *Adulterous Alliances.* Chicago: University of Chicago Press, 2000.

Hill, Christopher. "The Protestant Nation." *The Collected Essays of Christopher Hill Vol. 2.* Amherst: University of Massachusetts Press, 1986: 21–36.

Hunter, J. Paul. *Before Novels: The Cultural Contexts of Eighteenth Century English Fiction.* New York: W.W. Norton & Co., 1990.

Jordan, Constance. *Renaissance Feminism: Literary Texts and Political Models.* Ithaca: Cornell University Press, 1977.

Khanna, Lee Cullen. "No Less Real than Ideal: Images of Women in More's Work." *Moreana* 55–56 (1990): 35–51.

Levine, Joseph M. *Humanism and History: Origins of Modern English Historiography.*
    Ithaca: Cornell University Press, 1987.
Mitchell, Sally. *The Fallen Angel: Chastity, Class and Women's Reading 1835–1880.*
    Ohio: Bowling Green University Popular Press, 1981.
_____. "William Harrison Ainsworth." *Critical Survey of Long Fiction.* Edited by
    Frank N. Magill. Pasadena, Calif: Salem Press, 1991.
Morton, Gerald W. "The Two Faces of Eve: Thomas Heywood's Anne Frankford and
    Mrs. Wincott." *The Bulletin of the West Virginia Association of College English
    Teachers* 8 (Spring, 1983): 32–7.
Panek, Jennifer. "Punishing Adultery in *A Woman Killed With Kindness.*" SEL 34
    (Spring 1994): 357–79.
Pollak, Ellen. *The Poetics of Sexual Myth: Gender and Ideology in the Verse of Swift
    and Pope.* Chicago: University of Chicago Press, 1985.
Pratt, Samuel M. "Jane Shore and the Elizabethans: Some Facts and Speculations."
    Texas Studies in Literature and Language: A Journal of the Humanities, 11 (1970):
    1293–306.
Ross, Charles. *Edward IV.* New Haven: Yale University Press, 1974.
_____. *Richard III.* Berkeley: University of California Press, 1981.
Sanders, Andrew. *The Victorian Historical Novel—1840–*1880. New York: St. Martin's
    Press, 1979.
Schmidt, Roger. "Roger North's Examen: A Crisis in Historiography." *Eighteenth-
    Century Studies* 26:1 (Fall 1992): 57–75.
Shepard, Alan Clarke. "'Female Perversity,' Male Entitlement: The Agency of Gender
    in More's The History of Richard III." *Sixteenth-Century Journal* 26 (1995):
    311–28.
Smith, Henry. *A Preparation to Marriage.* London: Thomas Orwen for Thomas Man,
    1591.
Staznicky, Marta. "The End of Discord in *The Shoemakers' Holiday.*" *SEL* 36 (Spring
    1996): 357–73.
Strohm, Paul. *Hochon's Arrow: The Social Imagination of Fourteenth-Century Texts.*
    Princeton: Princeton UP, 1992.
Summers, Montague. *A Gothic Bibliography.* New York: Russell & Russell, 1964.
Sutherland, John. *Victorian Novelists and Publishers.* London: Athlone Press,
    1976.
Tanner, Tony. *Adultery in the Novel: Contract and Transgression.* Baltimore: Johns
    Hopkins University Press, 1979.
Tarvers, Josephine Koster. "'This Ys My Mystrys Boke': English Women as Readers
    and Writers in Late Medieval England." *The Uses of Manuscripts in Literary
    Studies: Essays in Memory of Judson Boyce Allen.* Penelope Reed Doob and
    Marjorie Curry Woods, eds. Studies in Medival Culture ser. 31. Kalamazoo:
    Western Michigan University, 1992: 305–27.
Thurston, Carol. *The Romance Revolution: Erotic Novels for Women and the Quest for
    a New Sexual Identity.* Urbana and Chicago: University of Illinois Press, 1987.

Traub, Valerie. *Desire and Anxiety: Circulation of Sexuality in Shakespearean Drama.* London: Routledge, 1992.

Watt, Tessa. *Cheap Print and Popular Piety, 1550–1640.* Cambridge Studies in Early Modern British History. Anthony Fletcher, series editor. Cambridge: Cambridge University Press, 1991.

Whately, William. *A Bride-Bush, or Wedding Sermon.* London, 1617.

Wood, James. "Madame Lewinsky: Or, Lord William's lover." *The New Republic,* 5 October 1998: 16–17.

Worth, George J. *William Harrison Ainsworth.* New York: Twayne, 1972.

Index

Aikins, Janet E. 72
Ainsworth, William Harrison 111–12,
    115 n.4, 115 n.5, 115 n.8, 115 n.19,
    117, 119, 120
  The Goldsmith's Wife 99–111
Appleyard, Susan 1, 119, 120, 121

Baines, Barbara J. 55, 56
Barker, Nicholas 2, 10, 11, 125, 126
Beith-Halami, Esther 4–5, 23, 36, 37
Belsey, Catherine 78
Bennett, Mrs. Mary 111, 115 n.4, n.13,
    n.15, n.16, n.19, 116 n.20
  Jane Shore: or, The Goldsmith's Wife
    98, 99–111
Birley, Sir Robert 129 n.3
Bleiler, E.F. 114, n.3
Booth, Michael 114
Born-Lechleitner, Ilse 67 n.8, 67 n.10,
    67 n.12, 67 n.14
Brett, Edwin James 98, 115 n.4
Budig, Willy 4

Charles I 69
Churchyard, Thomas 22, 28, 30, 31, 32,
    33, 36, 43, 45, 46, 54, 77, 119, 120
  "Howe Shore's Wife…" 22–8
Chute, Anthony 36, 46, 58
  "Bewtie Dishonoured…" 36–9
Costain, Thomas 7, 41
Croxall, Samuel 81, 86, 96
"Croyden Chronicle" 2

Dean, Leonard 16
Deloney, Thomas 28
  "A New Sonnet…" 28–30
Drayton, Michael 29, 31, 36, 39, 41, 42,
    43, 45, 57, 58
  "Edward the Fourth…" 39, 40–41

"The Epistle of Mistresss Shore…"
    39, 43–5

Edward IV 1, 8–10, 25, 126
Edward, prince of Wales, son of Henry
    VI 9
Elizabeth I 7, 21–2, 46

Freud, Sigmund 6 n.5

Gairdner, John 7
George, duke of Clarence 9–10
Gouge, William 24
Greenblatt, Stephen Jay 47 n.11
Grey, Thomas, marquis of Dorset 10,
    11, 19 n.3, 126–7
Guy, John 47 n.10

Harner, James 5, 21, 24, 86, 116 n.22,
    121
Hastings, William 10
Helgerson, Richard 3–4, 6 n.8, 66 n.1
Henrietta Maria, wife of Charles I 69
Henry VI 8–9
Henry, earl of Richmond, later Henry
    VII 9
Henry VIII 18, 21
Heywood, Thomas 16, 49, 72–3, 77
  *First and Second Parts of King
    Edward IV* 54–65, 66
Hill, Christopher 47 n.8
Howell, Jane
  Richard III 123
Hunter, Paul 71, 79, 87

John of Gaunt duke of Lancaster 8, 19
    n.2
Jordan, Constance 13

Khanna, Lee Cullen 15, 18

Lambert, John 10, 126, 127
Levine, Joseph M. 79
Lindsay, Philip 119, 120, 121
Loncraine, Richard 123, 125
Lukás, György 6 n.2
Lynom, Thomas 11, 127

Margaret of Anjou wife of Henry VI
    8–9, 111
Marotti, Arthur 42
McKellan, Ian 123, 125
Mitchell, Sally 111, 114 n.1, 115 n.4
Morand, Eugene, Vance Thompson and
    Marcel Schwob
    Jane Shore: a Drama in Five Acts
    118–19
More, Sir Thomas 1, 2, 3, 7, 10, 12, 23,
    25, 26, 27, 28, 30, 31, 38, 45, 46,
    50, 62, 79, 97, 118, 120, 126
    History of Richard III 12–19, 18, 21
Morton, Gerald W. 54
Muddock, J.E. Preston 1, 129 n.1

Nevill, Anne, daughter of earl of
    Warwick, later wife of Richard III
    9, 131 n.7
Nevill, Richard, earl of Warwick and
    Salisbury 8–9

Olivier, Laurence 121
    Richard III 121, 123

Paget, Guy 120, 121, 131 n.8
Paglia, Camille 89, 94 n.3
Panek, Jennifer 66 n.7, 67 n.13
Percy, Thomas 31, 66 n.6
Plaidy, Jean 120, 121
Pollak, Ellen 80
Pratt, Samuel M. 131 n.11

Rede, Lucy Leman
    The Monarch's Mistress 95–8

Richard, duke of Gloucester, later
    Richard III, brother of Edward IV 1,
    10–11, 127
Richard, duke of York, father of Edward
    IV, and Richard III 8, 11, 19 n.2
Richardson, Samuel 89
Ross, Charles 4, 6 n.6, 7, 8, 11, 12, 19
    n.4, 56, 61, 66 n.5, 67 n.9, 131 n.6
Rowe, Nicholas 1, 79, 86, 108, 121
    The Tragedy of Jane Shore 71–8
Rymer, Malcom James 111, 115 n.15,
    n.19
    *Jane Shore: or, London in the Reign
    of Edward IV* 98, 99–111

Sanders, Andrew 99, 115 n.8, 115 n.15
Schmidt, Roger 79
Seward, Desmond 7, 125–8, 131 n.10
Sewell, George 85, 96
Shakespeare, William 7, 12, 47 n.6, 51,
    54
    Richard III 49–51, 65, 66, 113, 116
    n.23, 121
Shepard, Alan Clarke 13
Shore, Elizabeth Lambert 10, 126, 127,
    129
Shore, William 10
Sidney, Sir Philip 42
Smith, Henry 29
Solmssen, Arthur 119, 120, 121, 131
    n.5, 131 n.9
Spenser, Edmund 89
Stallworth, Simon 10
Straznicky, Martin 66 n.4, 67 n.11
Strohm, Paul 19 n.5, 27, 46 n.2
Sutherland 115 n.6
Swynford, Katherine, second wife of
    John of Gaunt 8

Tanner, Tony 97
Tey, Josephine 7, 120
Thompson, C.J.S. 4, 115 n.17, 129 n.2

Thurston, Carol 129 n.4
Traub, Valerie 110
True Tragedie of Richard III 49, 51–4, 65, 66
Twayne 115 n.5

Vergil, Polydore 2, 11
Villiers, George, duke of Buckingham 69

Watt, Tessa 88
Whately, William 29
Wills, William Gorman 118, 121
   Jane Shore 112–14
"Wofull Lamentation…" 28, 31–5
Woods, James 128–9, 131 n.12
Woodville, Elizabeth, Lady Grey, wife of Edward IV 8, 12–13, 25, 34, 69

www.ingramcontent.com/pod-product-compliance
Ingram Content Group UK Ltd.
Pitfield, Milton Keynes, MK11 3LW, UK
UKHW020348010325
455677UK00021B/350